CREATIVE
TRESPASSING

CREATIVE
TRESPASSING

How to Put the Spark and Joy
Back into Your Work and Life

TANIA KATAN

CURRENCY
New York

Published in the United States by Currency, an imprint of the Crown
Publishing Group, a division of Penguin Random House LLC, New York.
currencybooks.com

CURRENCY and its colophon are trademarks of Penguin Random
House LLC.

A portion of this work was previously published by *Dame Magazine* in 2014.

Currency books are available at special discounts for bulk purchases for sales
promotions or corporate use. Special editions, including personalized covers,
excerpts of existing books, or books with corporate logos, can be created in
large quantities for special needs. For more information, contact Premium
Sales at (212) 572-2232 or e-mail specialmarkets@penguinrandomhouse.com.

Library of Congress Cataloging-in-Publication Data
Names: Katan, Tania, 1971–
Title: Creative trespassing : a totally unauthorized guide to unleashing your
    inner rebel and sneaking more imagination into your life and work /
    by Tania Katan.
Description: 1 Edition. | New York : Currency, [2018] | Includes
    bibliographical references and index.
Identifiers: LCCN 2018008909 | ISBN 9780525573401
Subjects: LCSH: Creative ability in business. | Success.
Classification: LCC HD53 .K38 2018 | DDC 650.1–dc23 LC record available
    at https://lccn.loc.gov/2018008909

ISBN 978-0-525-57340-1
Ebook ISBN 978-0-525-57341-8

Printed in the United States of America

Book design by Lauren Dong
Jacket design by Lucas Heinrich

10 9 8 7 6 5 4 3 2 1

First Edition

For the risk-taking misfits who are brave enough to write fight songs on company letterhead

CONTENTS

Creative Trespasser/cre-at-ive tres-pass-er/*noun*

1: Someone who sneaks creativity, imagination, and personality into the most mundane tasks or workplaces

2: Someone who defies conformity and disrupts the status quo to spark greater innovation and engagement in buttoned-up work environments

3: Someone who finds extraordinary ideas in ordinary places

4: Someone who uses creativity as fuel for a freer, more authentic life

Antonyms: paper pusher, corporate drone, desk jockey, mayor of Dullsville

NORMAL IS WHERE
CREATIVITY GOES TO DIE

Why fit in when you were born to stand out?

—DR. SEUSS

IT SEEMS FITTING that a book about disrupting business as usual should start with the ending. So, spoiler alert: I'm going to jump ahead and let you in on the punch line, the payoff, of this entire book. It's a little secret that NOBODY tells you, even though it's powerful and absolutely true: You don't need to turn into a corporate drone in order to kick ass in the working world. In fact, I'm here to tell you that you already *have* everything you need to stand out, take risks, and have a helluva lot of fun doing it. All you really have to do is trust your instincts, fire up your imagination, and stop apologizing for your magic and start unleashing it in the world! This book is about how.

It took me a long time to figure out that standing out was any kind of advantage, professional or otherwise, because I come from a long line of outsiders—people who didn't, and would never, fit in. For most of my young life I thought I had the suckiest DNA ever! Especially because the ONLY thing I wanted while growing up was to fit in. I wanted parents who had ordinary jobs, who packed snacks in my book bag each morning and ate dinner around an actual *table* at a certain time each night.

I wanted to live in a house, with married parents and maybe a dog, not a tiny apartment with one parent constantly on my case and the other parent on the lam.

I wanted a mother who wasn't a "foreigner" with a weird French accent and who didn't make me look up words in the dictionary because she didn't know English. I especially didn't want to have to look up and therefore learn phrases like "ends meet" and "Section 8 housing" and "out of work" at eight years old. I didn't want my mother to host parties full of artists and belly dancers and stinky French cheeses and jubilance. I didn't want my dad, a cabdriver, to have one more "big idea" that compelled him to bet on horses, enter into questionable "surefire" business ventures, or leave town unexpectedly for months or years on end. I wanted consistency. I wanted normal and I wanted it NOW. Only in hindsight would I discover that my outsider birthright and bizarro childhood were actually helping me chart my own course toward a wildly creative and fulfilling life.

When I was growing up and my single mom wasn't working two jobs as well as, in all her spare time, taking care of three unruly kids (sorry, Mom), she would take us to every arts and cultural event that started with *free* and ended in *festival*. And even though we had trouble making ends meet, Mom always found a little cash (usually stashed in her bra) to buy other people's art, and often even a little to buy art supplies for us. Mom understood that her creativity was a gift and figured out ways to make money with it. When our classmates attended summer camps we couldn't afford, Mom bartered her art-teaching skills in exchange for the camp letting my brother, sister, and me attend. To this day she still pays the guy who fixes broken stuff around her house with homemade quiche. Mom showed us that just about anything in life could be a creative pursuit and that we could find creativity anywhere we bothered to look for it.

My dad, on the other hand, had a true gift for figuring out creative ways to make money, namely, gambling. One of my father's glory stories was about the time he found himself down to his last hundred bucks. At that low point, most people would have filled out a job application, and then, you know . . . started working. Not my Pop. He gambled his life savings (yes, the whole $100) on a craps table in Laughlin, Nevada (couldn't even afford the real Vegas). Within twenty minutes of rolling the dice, Dad turned the last pennies he had to his name into a $500 jackpot. One could say that my father was the outsider pioneer of the "work smarter, not harder" movement. Or not. It's a fine line.

Between my mother's guiding philosophy—*creativity is currency!*—and my father's mantra—*why work a regular job when you can roll an eleven and quintuple your income in twenty minutes, all while enjoying a stiff cocktail on the house?*—I had no idea what making a viable living could possibly look like for me. Unlike my childhood peers, who had been given a clear formula for succeeding in life (high SAT scores + college + office job = success), my parents' instructions were all over the freaking map: *use your creativity, value imagination, question authority, gamble,* and, above all, *don't be ordinary.*

It would take me years to realize that my parents, in addition to enriching my future therapists, had accidentally taught me the hallmarks of success, innovation, joy, purpose, and everything else worth striving for in this world.

Still, it never occurred to me that standing out, breaking the mold, and marching to the beat of my own drum could actually be *cool* until I graduated from high school and enrolled in the misfit paradise known as theater school. As a boyish seventeen-year-old with little exposure to the thespian world (and even less to the lesbian world at that time), I had no idea that the theater nerds I was soon to meet would prove so validating of my nonconformist existence. In fact, the decision to go to theater school wasn't inspired by some lightbulb self-awareness moment, but rather by a field trip I took in grade school to see the play *Death of a Salesman*.

I know, weird, right? But that's what happened. As I stared down the barrel of what seemed to a seventeen-year-old me like the most momentous and life-defining decision I would ever face, the first thing that popped into my head was an image of Willy Loman, the ultimate conformist with his soul-sucking job, oversize gray suit, thinning hair, and air of utter desperation. He had made me feel something; he had moved me. In fact, that entire play had moved me . . . really far away from wanting to ever pursue a career in business. I mean, after seeing *that* rosy depiction of the place creativity goes to die, there was no way in hell I was gonna go anywhere near a major that might prepare me for a career in *the business world*. But theater, THAT was compelling. I wanted to move people too.

So, I applied for and was accepted into theater school. And that's when I found my fellow outsiders right there inside the theater department. We were the freaks and geeks who competed in speech and debate, scribbled ideas for plays on napkins, dressed in all black with accents of flannel (yes, the stereotype was true), and even had our own map for moving onstage: downstage, upstage, center stage, upstage left—which is really to the audience's right (still very confusing). In studying theater, I not only found my "tribe," I also learned how to see the blank page, the empty stage, the space between the beginning and the end, as full of possibilities.

Theater also showed me how to hone the skills and instincts I had inadvertently developed as a weirdo kid just trying to fit in. Growing up, I was often overlooked, left out, or picked last, if at all: whether because we were poor, because my parents were divorced, because my mom was an immigrant, or because of some other unspoken infraction of time and space, I couldn't say. Since fitting in hadn't come easily, if I wanted to connect with my classmates, I had to be creative about it. Theater too required drawing on creativity to make connections: to see patterns and symbols that weren't always obvious, to find new meaning, to overcome obstacles, and to conjure imagination wherever and whenever. When I was in grade school, I often had to develop novel ways to overcome bullies and get from point A to point B without getting picked on; putting on a play is all about overcoming obstacles and finding strategies to get from point A to point B—and if we're lucky, picking up a few epiphanies along the way. And theater helped to amplify the observation skills I'd picked up as a kid who was always relegated to watching from the sidelines. I became more adept at using my senses to assess a situation, adapt, collaborate, and create a bridge from idea to expression.

At twenty-one years old, I was on my way to becoming a pretty damn good playwright, and then I found a lump in my right breast. Long story short, I was diagnosed with breast cancer. And then, just as cancer had appeared out of nowhere and knocked the wind right out of me, inspiration, another unexpected visitor, struck suddenly (hey, nothing gets those creative juices flowing like surgery, chemotherapy, and hair loss!).

So, I put pen to paper and wrote the scenes of my life as they unfolded right in front of me. Pretty soon, the scenes added up to a full-length play that was produced around the country. Instead of cancer derailing my budding career as a playwright, it became the catalyst that launched it. Eventually, the cancer and I parted ways, my hair grew back, I learned to trust my body again, and it was time to leave university and jump into the workforce. And that's what I did, with the skills I had learned from theater (not to mention enduring cancer) in hand: resourcefulness, confidence, and the ability to turn whatever life threw at me into inspiration.

When I took these newly minted skills, along with my parents' quirky recipe for success, into the workforce I made two startling discoveries:

1. *Some people didn't give a crap about my creative bag-o-magic.*
2. *More people did!*

Although I desperately wanted to work as a full-time playwright while still living in Arizona, I knew those odds would not be in my favor. So, I packed up my bags, moved to San Francisco, and quickly learned that even there less than a thimble's worth of playwrights actually make a living writing plays.

I got a job bagging groceries, then worked in mom-and-pop coffee shops, after which I parlayed my coffee-making skills into jobs in office management, then made my way into print production, copywriting, and so on. All the while continuing to immerse myself in storytelling: writing plays, essays, and stories, seeing shows, absorbing all the ways in which artists were solving problems, conjuring imagination, and moving audiences from here to there.

And yet, no matter what tedium my work entailed—slinging coffee, bagging groceries, customer service, data entry, managing budgets, program planning, cold calling—I found a way to let creativity in. At first it was simply to keep myself entertained (and away from open windows), but soon people started noticing. Whether it was inviting fellow grocery store baggers to participate in playful challenges (*How many grumpy customers can you make smile today?*), writing custom plays for colleagues' birthdays and giving everyone in the department a part to read, coming up with snazzy names for elaborate coffee drinks, or simply engaging with colleagues to find out who they were, what they loved doing, and how they came to this work, my unconventional approaches to very conventional jobs began to earn me the attention, respect, and maybe even admiration of my buttoned-up supervisors, who didn't quite know what to make of the wacky office manager/barista/data clerk with the wild imagination who was breathing new life and energy into the staid office culture, but seemed to dig it.

Meanwhile, the more I was able to fuse imagination into these jobs, the more they started to feel like fun creative pursuits rather than crappy tasks. I felt just as much joy and energy balancing the program budget for a museum as I did writing a play for a theater company, just as much zeal for the challenge of remembering to place the eggs on top while bagging groceries as for memorizing my lines for a performance.

And this joy, this energy, this (at the risk of using a business buzzword) productivity was infectious. When my colleagues at the contemporary art museum, for example, saw me "executing the strategic objective of increasing audience attendance" by making funny videos, they realized that there could be more creative options for doing their own less technically "creative" work. In fact, at all of these jobs, my shenanigans inspired colleagues to start engaging in all kinds of seemingly mundane tasks with more imagination, gusto, and joy. I had to admit that ten-year-old me may have gotten it wrong. The business world might not be the place where creativity and imagination go to die, after all.

After more than ten years of smuggling creativity into the business sector without getting busted, I've learned that *we don't need to be in a job that is distinctly creative in order to be distinctly creative within our job.* No matter what we do or where we work, we can *all* transfer imagination into places where it doesn't seem to belong, but where it is desperately needed; where it adds layers that people never knew were missing in their lives but now can't live without.

This mindset that *any* pursuit can be a creative one has been my guiding principle ever since, and it's one that has allowed me to make an awesome living and life. This is the foundation for Creative Trespassing: the ability to conjure imagination in any place, at any time, knowing it will make you (and those around you) more innovative, more energized, and more valuable in your work and in the world!

WE DON'T NEED TO BE IN A JOB THAT IS DISTINCTLY CREATIVE IN ORDER TO BE DISTINCTLY CREATIVE WITHIN OUR JOB.

I know this because I've spent the last decade exploring the possibilities for sneaking creativity and imagination into the drabbest office environments, the most mundane daily tasks and routines, and the most rigid work practices. It all began, really, with the following questions: What if we brought our creative tools with us to the lobby? Our cubicle? The boardroom? Our everyday lives? Why do we feel like work and joy are mutually exclusive? What would happen if we infused ALL of ourselves into ALL of our work? Lest you think I was investigating these questions while stuffed into a lab coat and clinging to the certainty of a clipboard, rest assured, I was out in the field conducting the kind of renegade research that the business world might refer to as *batshit crazy*: I've driven four hundred miles to drop off a résumé because the job posting said "No phone calls, please"; gotten paid to encourage thousands of people to arm-wrestle in a museum; doubled my salary without permission; and jumped into a job that I was so woefully unqualified for that I had to do something EXTREME (you'll read about it later) in order to prove my value. The reviews were mixed. That's what happens when you nudge people and processes out of their comfort zones. Because the best ideas and innovations are rarely met with instant approval. In fact, mixed reviews are how you know you're on the right track!

After about five years of beta testing dozens of crazy, status-quo-busting practices, something totally unexpected happened. I was presented with a blank page and two plot points. I decided to test my unfolding methodology out on the challenge in front of me: to find the connective tissue between the two. The results were literally felt around the world.

It began with an unexpected call, and an even more unexpected proposal from a software company named Axosoft: They wanted to hire me as a brand evangelist. Holy shit! Software? I didn't know anything about technology (I had a flip phone, for realsies), plus I'm Jewish, so . . . evangelist?

Fast-forward to my third month on the job, and my boss asks me and a colleague to come up with an idea to address the issue of women in technology (more like the lack thereof). I saw a way to use my creative skills to create a campaign that would make people sit up and take notice; I would approach this tech problem with the analog mindset of a playwright and use storytelling as a way to dialogue. One of the biggest problems for women in tech was that they felt invisible, unheard, and discounted. So, I thought that if we could tell a story to help women feel *seen* in male-dominated fields like technology, maybe that would at least give them a fighting chance at narrowing that ginormous gender gap.

Eventually, I found inspiration in a place that in retrospect seems totally obvious, but simultaneously also completely unexpected: the sign hanging on the door of the women's bathroom. I took that familiar symbol hanging on doors of public restrooms worldwide, sketched a few lines along the sides of her triangle dress, and suddenly a superhero cape appeared.

As you'll read later on, the message of the campaign—*what if, instead of a dress, she was wearing a cape the whole time?*—was an invitation to see, hear, and celebrate women for the superheroes they are in the tech space and beyond. Basically, my ill-fitting skill set, coupled with small shifts in perspective and a gutsy collaborative team, helped birth an idea embraced by millions of people, companies, and movements globally as a symbol of empowerment and possibilities. That's what Creative Trespassing is all about: drawing on our unique perspective as "outsiders on the inside" to find extraordinary inspiration in those ordinary places where the best ideas, innovations, and magic reside.

I'm here to show you that even those of us who work in the most buttoned-up corporate environments can sneak more of our unbuttoned, untucked, uninhibited selves into our lives and work—and be rewarded for it. Because at a time when companies need disruptors and innovators more than ever, once we begin to celebrate the things that make us stand out, we can all truly shine. Whether it's by starting an innovation lab in our break room, translating your problem-solving skills from one field to another, or connecting two disparate ideas in order to find new meaning, we can all find ways to create more value for ourselves and our colleagues by igniting a creative revolution inside our body, mind, and cubicle.

Look, the reality is that we all can (and probably will) have the rug pulled out from under us at some point in our career. We might lose our job (thanks, robots), our cushy office with the great view, or even our crappy office with no view, the free pumpkin chocolate chip muffins in the break room, our spirit, and so on. But there's one thing NOBODY, not even the corporate overlords, can take away from us: our creativity. Just like snails carry their homes on their backs, we too can carry our creativity with us, wherever we go, wherever we work. You heard it here first: Creativity is the new job security.

Even though most of us instinctively know that using our creative skills can bring immense value to our lives, both at work and outside of it, at some point on our career path, many of us made a wrong turn. Do you remember? It was 102 degrees and you were trudging along the side of the dusty highway, lost, sweaty, super thirsty, wondering whether or not you would live to take another . . . arduous . . . step, and that's when you saw it! A fork in the road. Not the metaphor from that Robert Frost poem about a fork splitting the road into two different directions, but an animated dancing fork in the road, like a *Beauty and the Beast* fugitive, doing some Rockette-style kicks with its long cartoony tines. Remember? And then that dancing fork gestured for you to come a little closer, which of course you did because everyone knows that when a fork talks, you listen, right?! And then it asked you to make a decision. *Are you willing to give up all the stuff that makes you original, exceptional, and wonderfully weird in exchange for an average paycheck, regular hours, and the opportunity to watch your soul not die, but atrophy slowly, every day, for the rest of your life? What say you?*

And you know what you said? Nothing! Because there is no animated dancing fork in the middle of the desert—unless you are high (I don't judge)! And there is no metaphorical fork forcing you to choose between career stability and a life of creativity and joy. That fork doesn't exist. I made it up, just like society made up the idea that we can't stay true to our wacky, unique self if we want to "make it" in the professional world. That notion is a mirage brought to us by years of schooling, well-meaning parents and friends, the media, the old guard, and the letter O, as in *Oh shit, I have a choice?*

You do have a choice, but it's a very different one. You can keep plugging along in your job, keep playing by the rules and following the script . . . OR you can use your imagination to get unstuck. That's exactly where Creative Trespassing comes in.

Maybe you picked up this book because you've lost your verve, your drive, your way—and you want your freaking spark back between the hours of nine and five. Maybe you're an entrepreneur seeking new ways to innovate, to turn your big dreams and bigger ideas into reality. Maybe you're a paper pusher wishing to transform monotony into novelty, apathy into alchemy. Maybe you're an assistant or an intern waiting in the wings for your turn to share a creative idea. Maybe you're an entry-level person doing menial work but dreaming of meaningful work. Maybe you're a manager or exec who made a devil's pact with the universe ("If I promise to give up painting, will you hook me up with a regular paycheck and a job title that doesn't embarrass my mother?"). Maybe you're a free spirit with a rich creative life outside the office looking to bring more of that magic into your job. Or maybe you're just someone who believes that you have a greater purpose and calling on this planet, who knows that life is short, so why waste one minute of it complaining about your job? This is a book for anyone stuck in cubicles, mindsets, wide neckties, or ill-fitting pencil skirts (or all of the above). It's for everyone who has ever felt the urge to scream, "Why does it say paper jam when there is no paper jam?!!"

Hey, I've been stuck in that cubicle, in that mindset, and, yes, even in a much-too-wide necktie (please don't close your eyes and imagine it), and I've lived to tell the story! How? Because I've chosen to stand out rather than fit in, to find my light and bask in it with all of my flaws, scars, foibles, and polyester work costumes. The moment you choose to let the world see the real you—messy, imperfect, warts and all—is the moment you choose to shine too.

If this talk of letting it all hang out there, warts and all, is starting to scare you, remember this: Anything worth doing resides on the corner of Challenging and Necessary, which is just down the street from Terrified and Excited (this ain't your grandpappy's gated community).

It's okay, I get freaked out about starting something that's challenging and necessary too. Every. Single. Time. Every consulting project, every speech, every time I feel that unmistakable urge to let my craziest ideas, my innermost monologue, my deepest secrets loose into the world—hell, sometimes even grocery shopping—scares the living daylights out of me. And then I look on my refrigerator to see the poem I placed there in case of an existential emergency, "The Summer Day" by Mary Oliver. The last line of poem is "Tell me, what is it you plan to do with your one wild and precious life?" Oh, it gets me every time. Because this is it, kids. I don't mean to get all life-or-deathsy here, but regardless of what your beliefs are about death or life or life after death, why *would* you want to squander a single moment of your one wild and precious life?

THE MOMENT YOU CHOOSE TO LET THE WORLD SEE THE REAL YOU— MESSY, IMPERFECT, WARTS AND ALL— IS THE MOMENT YOU CHOOSE TO SHINE TOO.

As you move through this book, you'll be asked to declare your passions, trust your instincts, and give yourself unlimited permission to make your mark in this lifetime and beyond (creative legacy, baby). In the pages ahead I'll show you how to jump into uncharted territory and plot a wild and precious life inside and outside of work that makes your day-to-day grind feel like painting, like singing, like dreaming, like flying, like being alive. This book will give you the tools to infuse imagination even in the darkest places, and to reconnect with your inspiration even when it seems like the last thing on your to-do list. It will give you permission to rebel against the status quo and color outside the lines to breathe new energy and life into people and places in need of a shot in the arm. It will ask you to dream big and take small, maybe even baby, steps toward bringing those dreams to life. This book is an invitation to ban the words "I should" from your vocabulary and map the most kick-ass life you desire.

Along the way, I'll share the secrets of my successes, along with my many mishaps, foibles, and downright awkward attempts to bring creativity into less overtly creative spaces and situations. And I'm going to hook you up with stories, examples, and perspectives you probably won't find in any other business book. In the spirit of exploring all the stuff outside, on the fringes, to bring more just-crazy-enough-to-work ideas inside, you'll learn about artists and cultural change-makers you might have never heard of. And, on the flip side, some totally legit business leaders you might know of who have agreed to share their most daring and rule-breaking insights and exploits with me—and you.

I've had the privilege of learning from some of the most brilliantly subversive—and totally under-the-radar—Creative Trespassers of our time, and I'm not afraid to share their secrets with you. People like the choreographer Elizabeth Streb, who has merged her love of physics and math with dance to explore the question *Can we fall up?* Like my buddy Elizabeth Cutler, who spun her expertise in ditching work with her business savvy into the monster fitness brand SoulCycle. And plenty of people not named Elizabeth too!

And once you see how powerful (and easy) Creative Trespassing can be, you're gonna want to start trespassing too! This will require busting up some norms and sneaking into unauthorized spaces and situations to inspire more responsible and necessary rule breaking. We're talking scaling imaginary walls that we erect between desks, departments, and disciplines to find inspiration where others see only limitations.

THIS BOOK IS AN INVITATION TO BAN THE WORDS "I SHOULD" FROM YOUR VOCABULARY AND MAP THE MOST KICK-ASS LIFE YOU DESIRE.

So, are you ready to learn how? We're just going to start with the rules. Nothing to worry about. Rules are safe and snuggly, right? At this point you might be thinking, *Hold the phone, rules? That doesn't sound very rebellious.* But here's the deal: Only once we know the rules can we know when to break, follow, or reinvent them. Just like stage directions give actors a starting point from which to explore the world around them, rules give us the starting point from which we chart our own course. Rules give us plot points to help orient us. They give us a structure to explore, to resist, to push up against, to bend, to break, and to locate our place within. Rules show us what's possible. This is critical, because we often forget that we need to see what is possible so we can create the impossible; that in order to reimagine something we have to imagine it first. So here we have it:

RULES OF CREATIVE TRESPASSING

RULE #1: **Fear Is So Last Year**

In the face of dread, avoidance, and inertia . . . begin. Push yourself out of your comfort zone to create something unique and new and wonderful. Surprise yourself.

RULE #2: **Transform the Norm**

When faced with the choice between originality or conformity, always take the road less traveled. Dare to defy conventions and challenge the status quo. Disrupting the systems that keep us stuck leads to more joy, happiness, and freedom (even at work).

RULE #3: **Take Permission—'Cause No One Is Gonna Give It to You**

Stealing permission in service of your dreams is totally legal. Who's going to stop you? The permission cops? They ain't real. Your dreams are, so go in hot pursuit of them.

RULE #4: **Let Your Freak Flag Fly**

Celebrate the stuff that makes you stand out! Champion calamities, flaws, and profoundly awkward moments, knowing that these are where the best art, ideas, innovations, and experiences live!

RULE #5: **Suspend Disbelief**

Leave logic and limits behind. Investigate what is possible, probable, profitable. Then ask yourself, "What if the truth were, in fact, the opposite?" Jump, defy gravity, and let your inner caped crusader take flight.

RULE #6: **Ditch School**

Know the rules. Then question them. Escaping the office and getting out into the world to wander is a surefire way to find your spark.

RULE #7: **Think Inside the Box**

Sneak your creativity into confined spaces, no matter how tiny, then break down the walls to make room for ideas that have no bounds. The less imaginative our physical office—or our job or title or role—the *more* essential our imagination becomes.

RULE #8: **Lose the Map, Find Your Sense of Direction**

Get lost and find your own way of getting from here to there. Practice radical compassion and let your values and convictions guide your road less traveled from purpose to plan.

RULE #9: **Unleash Your Inner Rebel**

Challenge rigid notions of business as usual with all the rebellious curiosity of a rule-breaking outsider. Adopt the following as your battle cry: *Creativity is an act of defiance!*

RULE #10: **Kick Imposter Syndrome in the Arse**

Call bullshit on self-doubt. Trust that you've done your homework, developed your skills, and are ready to rock the house.

RULE #11: **Outgrow Adulting**

Imagine life without imagination. Impossible! Use imagination to explore what's possible and then reimagine it. Believe in the power of make-believe and harness the creativity of your wild inner child.

RULE #12: **Turn into the Skid**

Dare to stare everyday annoyances, challenges, and expectations in the eye and barrel headfirst into them with courage, curiosity, and creativity. Make resilience a personal best practice.

RULE #13: **Crash the Company Picnic**

Our gutsiest shenanigans are often our greatest differentiators. Find unconventional applications for the skills you leave off your résumé and use your powers of sneakery to bring them into work.

RULE #14: **Level Up Your Listening**

In the chaos and noise that often underscores our lives, we need space to listen to our thoughts, make connections, and let our imaginations run wild. Resist the urge to fill up empty spaces. Instead, listen for the music in the silence and make room for the invisible to become visible.

RULE #15: **Resuscitate Your Work Culture, for Art's Sake**

Breathe new life into dusty procedures, processes, and practices. Turn to the arts, and other unexpected places, to make your culture state of the art.

RULE #16: **Fire Hierarchy**

Crack the veneer of status and job title to inspire change, action, and collaboration. Recognize people's unique abilities and give everyone a chance to come onstage and grab the mic.

RULE #17: **Reframe the Blame**

When the well of excuses runs dry, that's when you experience a wellspring of creativity. Choose to let go and be free.

RULE #18: **Turn Your Vocation into a Vacation**

We often think of vacations as the only times we get to truly reflect, learn, and explore. It's time to bring that sense of wonder, thirst for adventure, and focused serenity to work. When your vocation gives you limes, adopt a vacation mindset and make margaritas.

RULE #19: **If All Else Fails . . . Keep Rehearsing**

All "instant" successes were years in the making. Take a risk, gather feedback, practice, launch, repeat. Success is the act of trying in the face of failure.

RULE #20: **Pay ~~Your Dues~~ Attention**

When starting out in a creative career, you may have to do stuff that seems less creative. But when you start paying attention to the tasks that seem like busy-work, you'll discover golden opportunities to learn. When the drudgery of paying your dues feels like it's robbing you of your imagination, don't just grit your teeth and bear it. Turn it into inspiration instead.

RULE #21: **Show Up**

. . . and bring your magic and good humor with you, everywhere you go. Find and use your unique voice in the service of elevating your fellow human beings. Let relentless curiosity be your guide as you forge a unique path toward a totally kick-ass life!

SO LET'S GET STARTED, knowing that the rewards are many and that the payoff can be incredible.

What are you waiting for? Permission? It's time to open a can of whoop-ass on permission! If I had waited for permission, there is no way I'd be where I am today: traveling the world speaking, consulting, coaching, writing. My life is delightfully unauthorized; I'm authoring it as I go.

So, the only question is: Do you want to be the author of your own life? Are you ready to bridge the space in between *work* and *life*; between *creativity* and *deliverables*; between *what we do* and *who we are*? Are you ready to take a step outside your comfort zone—then another, and another? Are you ready to learn how to use creativity as the fuel for a freer and more authentic life?

CHAPTER 1

FEAR IS SO
LAST YEAR

I can't understand why people are frightened of
new ideas. I'm frightened of the old ones.

—JOHN CAGE, *Avant-garde Composer*

AT NINETEEN YEARS OLD I heard my calling, a clear message
delivered from above. The voice was not God's or my guardian angel's. Rather, it belonged to the tall, stern undergraduate adviser informing me that, "The only playwriting class we
have available is for graduate students. You're an undergraduate.
You could submit a piece of writing and try to get in, but your
chances are slim."

Sure, many people in my position may have taken this as bad
news, but I've always been a fan of slim chances. In fact, if chances
are too chubby, I tend to give up before I even start. It's a trait I
inherited from my father, the OG underdog, who used to buy
lottery tickets only when the jackpot was good and fat and worth
(in his mind) the time and energy it took for him to sip scotch at
a neighborhood bar while slowly scratching off the silver coating
covering the numbers with the edge of a thin dime. He usually
won a buck or two—one time he even won a few hundred—but
for my dad, it wasn't about winning the big jackpot, it was about
the *anticipation*, about getting pleasantly day drunk while ponder-

ing the possibility of winning against all odds. In fact, the more the odds were stacked against him, the more fun for him it was.

So, chip off the old block that I was, I ignored my adviser's advice and decided to play the odds with a satirical poem I'd written about pretentious folks who performed poetry in coffee-houses entitled "I Wear Black! And You Don't."

The first line: "YOU, like the bug / at the bottom / of my Big Gulp . . ."

The last line: "I slit my wrists horizontally as opposed to vertically and laugh. Ha. Ha. Ha. I wear black! And you don't."

As it turned out, I had much better luck than my father, because, somehow, not only did I not get put on suicide watch, I won the jackpot: a spot in the graduate playwriting class. On the first day of the semester I was so excited I practically skipped into the classroom. I couldn't believe my good fortune. *No more slumming it with the undergrad crowd for me*, I thought as I found a seat next to a woman who was hunched over her notebook, scribbling furiously. *I'm in the big leagues now!*

There were only seven of us in the class, and the graduate students were all decked out in the fashion of the time—grunge, some combination of black T-shirts with flannel accents, worn-out jeans, dirty sneakers, and a studied air of gloominess. Whereas my outfit—large silver hoop earrings (jutting out from short spiky hair) and pale pink button-down oxford (although in my defense, it *was* untucked from my light blue jeans)—was giving off a vibe that was more "professional lesbian golfer" than "future Tony Award–winning playwright." They all seemed to have the same notebooks, you know, those nineties-looking ones with the black and white blotches on the cover. My notebook, on the other hand, was more of an assertive orange (some might have said fluorescent, but same difference). *Don't worry about it*, I assured myself. *You belong here. These are your peeps.*

The first several minutes of class passed in eerie silence, as though the other writers were communicating telepathically in some secret language I didn't speak. Finally, the professor, who had been busy emptying the mysterious contents of his worn brown leather satchel onto his desk, sat down, faced us, and delivered his marching orders: "There are three people stuck in a moving vehicle. Go!" All six sophisticated, flannel-clad grad students quickly cracked open their identical notebooks, put pen to paper, and started moving their hands as if the divine spirit of next-level-shit playwriting had suddenly entered their bodies. The spirit seemed to have skipped over me, however, and instead sent his friend, the divine spirit of holy-crap-what-is-happening. I was frozen. Couldn't move a muscle. I let out a vague squeak, like the Tin Man begging for a tune-up, and leaned in to ask the professor in a stage whisper, "Are we writing a play? Is that what we're doing here?"

He nodded in the affirmative, which most people would have taken as a cue to start writing, but I could only sit there, utterly paralyzed. I was stuck. I'd been in class for all of five minutes, and I had writer's block already?? Fear filled my entire being as my brain began generating involuntary "what if"s. *What if I can't think of anything to write? What if my writing sucks? What if the grad students make fun of me? What if they find out I'm a playwriting imposter? What if I spontaneously combust?*

For lack of any better options, I put pen to blank page and started writing the stage directions that all plays begin with, *lights up to reveal* . . . And then the weirdest thing happened. I kept writing. In fact, my hand didn't stop moving until the professor yelled, "Time's up. Hand in your plays." That's when I realized that I had written, nonstop, for fifty-five minutes! It felt like being high, only with more focus and less munchies. And the craziest part: The play was actually good. I know this because the professor called me into his office the next day and said, "Tania, this play is actually good." Followed by the words I had previously heard only in my wildest dreams: "You should submit it to playwriting contests."

I tell this story not to brag about my innate playwriting talent (okay, maybe just a little), but rather because how I began that day, sitting in that classroom blinded by the glare of the white, empty pages of my weird orange notebook staring back at me, is how everyone—every performer, painter, software developer, manager, educator, cashier, dog walker, flight attendant—starts the day: facing an empty stage, a blank page, a bare canvas, a napping computer screen, an unfamiliar route, the clear, open sky. Whether we work in a soul-sucking corporate job or at the coolest "creative job" ever (or someplace in between), we all start each day from scratch. But here's the amazing thing about the proverbial blank page: We get to choose how to fill it. We get to decide whether what we put on that page will be conventional, expected, and safe, or whether it will be daring, audacious, and wildly creative.

We get to choose whether to stare blankly at the white emptiness, praying for the divine spirit of creativity to swoop in and start making out with us, or whether to trust that there is an entire world waiting to be explored in that space, put pen to paper, and *start*. To make a mark, a simple act that might inspire us to make another mark, and then another, and pretty soon the sum total will add up. Ultimately, when faced with that proverbial blank page, we can either begin to write or allow inertia to keep us stuck in the thick smog of fear and self-doubt. It's *our* choice to make anew every day.

WE GET TO DECIDE
WHETHER WHAT WE PUT ON THAT PAGE WILL BE CONVENTIONAL,
EXPECTED, AND SAFE, OR WHETHER IT WILL BE DARING, AUDACIOUS, AND WILDLY CREATIVE.

Fear of the blank page strikes the most creative among us. Like the artist Maurizio Cattelan who, in the eighties, was on the verge of his first-ever solo exhibition, one that would launch his art career and . . . he couldn't think of anything to make. He was too consumed by freaking out; totally paralyzed by the fear, anxiety, and insecurity over creating and displaying his art. And his gallery, well, they were no help. The organizers of the event weren't about to move the date just because the artist was feeling stuck. They didn't give a shite about his creative block. The show was gonna go on whether Mr. Cattelan was scared to make his mark or not. As his exhibition grew closer, Cattelan grew even more riddled with anxiety, which left him even less inspired to create than before (which was NOT AT ALL). So he did the only thing he could think of, which was: to run for the hills . . . like, NOW.

So, it's opening night and what does he do? He closes the gallery and hangs a sign on the door that reads *Torno subito*, or "Be right back." And get this: The art world loved it! They immediately understood that the sign was an admission of the fear and anxiety we all feel when we have to show our work; they saw the sign as a statement about the very nature of art. Instead of making objects to show in the gallery, Cattelan leaned into his fear and turned it into actual artwork. From that day forward, Cattelan never ran away from an exhibition again, no matter how stuck he got, and he has since gone on to enjoy a tremendously successful career as an artist because, in his words, he makes art "about the impossibility of doing something . . . about insecurity, about failure."

And that, m'friends, is what being a Creative Trespasser is all about. Facing our fears, anxieties, and impending D-day moments and turning them into works of art. With our imagination and creativity ignited, we can make something out of anything, even if that anything is nothing. And this is true whether we are facing a looming art exhibition, a new job, a big project or account or presentation, or anything else. Taking a blank page and filling it with something unique and new and wonderful: That's the job of the Creative Trespasser.

At this point you might have some of the same questions that people often ask me when I give talks about Creative Trespassing, for example: "How can I break the rules and fill my blank page, as it were, if I work in the most conservative company? I traded my soul for a key fob, a 401(k), and golden handcuffs."

I feel you. I've worn some pretty tight handcuffs and even tighter company logo shirts, and I know that a cubicle can feel like a gray, fluorescent-lit prison of your own making. But the good news is that we *can* shake off, or at least loosen, those corporate shackles and disrupt the conventions even in the most conventional environment; we just gotta do it acoustic style: that is, no amps, unplugged, and under the radar. That's why the acts of creative sneakery in this book come in a variety of shapes, sizes, and styles. Only you can be the judge of what will fly in your company, so it's up to you to choose the acts that will get you and your colleagues' imaginations fired up—without getting you fired.

Here's another question I hear all the time: *What if I get pushback? What if my ideas get pushed down?*

If you are successfully disrupting the status quo in your workplace, you will absolutely get pushback and pushed down. Sorry. But the truth is that there will always be people, teams, and entire departments that will respond to your courage, creativity, and care with proportionate fear, reluctance, and eye rolling.

And, yeah, it stings for a few seconds, but then, without fail, the sting gives way to a smile: You survived. The more you engage in Creative Trespassing, the more you'll see pushback as a sign that you are doing exactly what you are meant to be doing: nudging people out of their comfort zones, breathing new life into the company culture, and igniting a creative revolution in the workplace that will ultimately lead to more exciting innovations, more authentic connections, and deeper insights.

CHAPTER 2

TRANSFORM
THE NORM

Creativity is an act of defiance.

—TWYLA THARP, *Dancer and Choreographer*

THE FIRST BOARD GAME I ever remember playing as a kid was Chutes and Ladders. It was for the preschool set, so there were no words on the game board, just pictures of little kids engaged in various activities that were deemed either a "Good Behavior," like doing chores, or a "Bad Behavior"—which was usually something surely forbidden, like drawing on the wall with a crayon. Landing on a Good Behavior square meant you could ascend the ladder. A Bad Behavior would shoot your shit down a chute faster than you could say "I wanna go to art school!"

As a kid, these classifications of "good" and "bad" always puzzled me—and, to be honest, they still do. Most of those mischievous activities didn't seem so bad; in fact, some of them were downright creative and fun. There was the kid riding a bicycle with his hands and feet in the air, smiling as the wind blew through his hair. Another was drawing a mural of stars and lightning bolts. Another was actually reading a book! And one was carefully carrying a stack of dishes (probably to help her mom, because her dad was at the racetrack losing their rent money). Sure, the dishes slipped out of her hands and smashed into smithereens, but that wasn't her fault! It ended equally badly for all of them. You can imagine my horror when I, as a curious three-year-old, witnessed the fate of those inquisitive kids.

It's astounding that a game meant for children would send this kind of message: that a child's curious nature should be punished. What if, instead of giving the kid riding the bike a broken arm, they gave him a cape and he became Evel Knievel? What if, instead of giving the little girl coloring on the wall a sponge and a look of shame, they gave her a canvas and she became Frida Kahlo? What if the little girl balancing a thousand plates made it to the kitchen and became the next Julia Child?

What if, instead of getting busted up for breaking the rules, these kids were rewarded for rebelling against conformity and boredom?

Of course, the game is just a symptom of the larger problem: Many of us are raised to believe that if we dare to play, to create, or to explore, we better be prepared to suffer the consequences. Unfortunately, this message is only reinforced once we become adults and enter the workforce. Now we get to trade our crappy Chutes and Ladders in for the Corporate Ladder—an even higher-stakes game where breaking the rules, we are led to believe, has even greater consequences. But does it? NO. As Creative Trespassers we know that "'good behavior" means breaking some rules to create more opportunities for unfiltered expression, audacious contributions, and childlike curiosity!

It wasn't until the sixth grade that I fully grasped this concept. This was a time when I was the only girl on the boys' basketball team, had my hair cut—by my mother—in a pioneering avant-garde style that can best be described as a forerunner to the mullet, and was obsessed with Culture Club, more specifically Boy George, to the point that I was prone to repeating "Tania George" over and over again—aloud. This was also around the

time when I began practicing homespun stand-up comedy routines in my bedroom with a hairbrush for a microphone that I
would tap (before starting my "set") before asking my imaginary
audience, "Is this thing on?" I'm not gonna lie, I was cool beyond
my years. I was, if you will, an early beta test of me. And like
many great inventions that emerge ahead of their time—the internet, self-driving cars, Pampers for adults—mainstream society
wasn't ready to understand or accept my supreme coolness.

At every turn there seemed to be a reluctant early adopter
of me more than happy to push me down a chute as punishment for daring to go against the grain. Sometimes, it was for
breaking an official rule of the school, like the time I landed
a week's worth of detention for calling a classmate the F word
(for the record, she started it). And other times it was for breaking one of the unspoken rules, like having no friends. It wasn't
like I *wanted* no friends. I totally wanted friends. Unfortunately,
the school bully, Cathie, thought my infraction was worthy of
punishment anyway and would frequently enforce the unwritten
laws of schoolyard etiquette through shoving and other forms
of violence. Throughout that year, whenever I'd ask my mom
whether I'd ever fit in, she'd tell me not to worry. "You're just a
late bloomer," she'd explain while trimming my sideburns. In
fact, I had both of my less-than-conventional parents coaching
me from the sidelines, telling me to use my voice, practice non-
violence, and be myself. With that advice, I dropped a "Karma
Chameleon" on my record player and waited to blossom (and
waited and waited and . . .).

I now realize that in sixth grade (and all grades leading up
to it) I wasn't a "bad kid"; I was an accidental disruptor. Meaning that I wasn't *trying* to be a nonconformist; in fact, I was
trying to fit in. My strategy: being myself. *Be yourself* was the
refrain I had heard over and over—from my parents, teachers,

Marlo Thomas's album *Free to Be . . . You and Me*, and ABC after-school specials—so I assumed that was the only way to be. Which sounds cool and fun now, but at the time it was a huge problem given that "being myself" more or less guaranteed that I would very conspicuously stick out.

And the more I tried to fit in, the more my disruptive nature was determined to shine through. At the time, this sucked more than a pile of rotten eggs, but as it turned out, the nonconformist ethics I'd learned from my mom and in the schoolyard—*approach typical questions atypically, lead with good humor, find your voice and use it,* and *be yourself*—would end up serving me quite well later in life. When you're in the sixth grade, standing out generally gets you kicked in the shins; but in the working world, it gives you a huge leg up. At a time when businesses are more obsessed with innovation than ever, there are a lot of reasons why it's good to stand out, to be noticed, to be a disruptor: It makes you memorable, it helps people see you as a leader, and it makes you a valuable asset to any team seeking different or unique perspectives. Being unconventional, in other words, makes you indispensable.

Once I entered the workforce, my unique voice helped me land jobs at companies trying to develop compelling brands, voices, and stories. Using good humor allowed me to collaborate successfully with some very difficult personalities. In brainstorming sessions, my atypical questions have often sparked fresh ideas and outcomes. Even saying the F word, every once in a while, let potential clients know that I wasn't afraid of taking on edgier projects. In short, my natural inclination toward standing out has afforded me many kick-ass opportunities to collaborate, innovate, and captivate—and inspire others to do the same.

Today, defying convention is literally my vocation. But just in case you think I disrupt for the hell of it, or the yell I get, or the smell of it, I can assure you: Companies actually hire me—voluntarily!—to come in and shake up the way they work.

That's because smart companies know that disruption creates more opportunities to learn, heal, and grow. They know that employees who are encouraged to find their voice and use it, bring their authentic selves to work, and approach their jobs with curiosity and joy are not only less disgruntled, but also more productive. And they know that the more their colleagues defy convention and expectations, dare to challenge the norms, and force themselves to step outside of their comfort zones, the more innovative, competitive, and profitable they are.

Not to mention the fact that everyone is talking about the benefits of diversity in business. Not just in the traditional sense, but as in diversity of thought and perspective. Smart companies are finally figuring out that if they really want to cultivate a culture of diverse people, ideas, questions, and actions, then they have to stop rewarding conformity and groupthink and start inviting diverse people, ideas, questions, and actions into the fold.

While the word *disruption* might conjure images of disorder and chaos, the reality is that more thoughtful disruptions lead to more fruitful and productive work. That's why throughout the book you'll encounter mini-exercises that I call Productive Disruptions; these suckers are here to give you a shot of inspiration as you seek and find your own respectfully subversive ways to transform the norms in your workplace. Because when we disrupt the status-quo systems and processes keeping people stuck, we actually produce more generative collaborations and teamwork, greater focus and engagement, and more empathetic and authentic communication—all of which lead to more innovative ideas and breakthroughs. True story. News at ten.

So, the next time you're faced with the choice between creativity or convention, originality or normality, using your voice or shutting your mouth, letting go or pushing back, I want you to have the tools and confidence to choose the road less traveled. Your employers will notice you (in a good way), your teams will thank you, and you will thank you because you have chosen the road that encourages you to shine, thus creating a platform for everyone else to shine too. Plus, take it from me: Life as a nonconformist is a lot more freeing, fascinating, and effing fun.

Here are a couple of ways to defy and disrupt workplace norms that actually work.

LIFE AS A NONCONFORMIST IS A LOT MORE FREEING, FASCINATING, AND EFFING FUN.

READ THE WRITING ON THE WALL

Whenever I'm invited to give talks at start-ups, universities, or corporations about embracing a diverse work culture and empowering women to enter STEAM (science, technology, engineering, art, and math) fields, I'm always given a tour of the facilities. The first stop is usually the wall-o-quotes: you know, those inspiring displays of borrowed wisdom that have been carefully curated to ignite the next gen of industry disruptors.

And about 98 percent of the time, about 98 percent of the quotes are from dudes. Mostly white dudes. I can only assume that the people who hung them there didn't give much thought to the fact that if a company wants its employees to embrace diversity, it might be a good idea to display a little diversity. In the wise words of Kimberly Bryant, founder of Black Girls Code, "You can't be it if you can't see it."

Glaring disconnects like these are always clear signs that a brand's stated values and realities are out of alignment. Having worked with companies and start-ups in many industries, from health care to higher education to software, I know how hard it can be to maintain a connection between brand promise and brand delivery, especially when scaling a company or idea. This is why it's important for those of us on the ground, us Creative Trespassers, to speak up when the promise writ large on the wall—or, for that matter, on the company website or any other communication to employees and customers—is out of whack with the company's overall expression.

I once belonged to a gym that had profoundly terrible customer service. When I would approach the desk to check in, I was never greeted with a "Hello" or "Welcome" or "What's up?" Just one or more grumpy-looking employees glued to their phones or in deep conversation with coworkers who couldn't be bothered to look up. The employees at the front desk always looked so unhappy, you'd think they were working in a sweatshop. Well . . . I guess technically they were, but still. The point is, it's not manual labor, it's a customer service job.

One day, while checking into said gym, I looked up to discover a giant sign on the wall displaying the company's brand promise writ large: IT'S THE WAY WE MAKE YOU FEEL. And right underneath it, as if the gym had signed up to host a new season of *Big Brother*, was a surveillance camera.

In an effort to be a customer of service, I shared my observation with a customer service rep at the front desk. "Isn't that ironic? A sign that claims you want to make us feel welcome hanging right next to a security camera menacingly watching our every move?"

Apparently, he didn't see the irony. But Creative Trespassers see signs like these as opportunities to start conversations, to heal issues, to disrupt the norms that are at odds with what the company stands for.

Productive Disruption

1. Go on a self-guided tour of your company's walls (and/or website).
2. Find the tension between the company's promises (quotes, mission statement, vision, etc.) and the on-the-ground realities.
3. Brainstorm ways to draw attention to the contradiction and encourage cultural shifts that will help bring everyday activities into alignment with the values of the company.
4. Use humor. Here's a slide I quickly added to a talk after being given the 98 percent tour: "Hey, I'm a big fan of dudes—my dad is one, lots of my friends are, and my brother is a dude too! Alas, diversity in the workforce has been proven to give companies the competitive edge, so . . . Got Diverse Quotes?" The slide got a hearty if somewhat sheepish laugh and generated an awesome conversation during the Q&A!

Sometimes there isn't *any* writing on the company's walls: no quotes, no art, nothing but chipped paint and bad lighting, kinda like the joint just barely survived the zombie apocalypse— but scarier because it's your workplace. In this case, take matters into your own hands. Come up with a list of inspiring and diverse quotes, or poetry, or anything else you think appropriate and would stick on the wall. If you're feeling really daring . . . hang back after hours and do it rogue style.

BE THE CHARACTER (DON'T JUST PLAY THE PART)

Russian theater director and teacher Konstantin Stanislavski was a productive disruptor in the world of theater who blew up the prevailing acting methodologies by training actors to *embody* the character, rather than *pretend to be* the character. Instead of approaching the role thinking, "The character is sad? Okay, I will frown and mope around the stage. I will act sad," Stanislavski encouraged actors to access their own "emotional memories" for experiences similar to the character's. This allowed them to actually feel what that character might be feeling, thus *becoming* a character onstage rather than a stiff representation of one.

In the business world, there are still plenty-o leaders approaching their roles by playing a character rather than embodying one. "I'm a CEO? Okay, I will be stern, pretend I know everything, and boss my subordinates around so they know their role and mine." The problem with this approach is that to succeed in the business world today, we need to start understanding and absorbing the inner landscapes of our customers, colleagues, and work cultures, something that's hard to do if we're always trying to act a role we believe is prescribed for us based on our rank or job title.

My friend Sherry Cameron, CEO, company founder, and a licensed psychologist who works with people and companies in crisis, uses a highly creative variation of Stanislavski's methodology to help colleagues and teammates gain a deeper understanding of one another. Instead of swooping in and making blanket evaluations of people based on templated criteria, Sherry sits down with every team member and talks with them. You know, like they are human beings. She asks them how and why they do what they do in the company; she gets them talking about their challenges and aspirations. She gets to know them in an authentic way. Then she presents each team member with a hat filled with folded pieces of paper. They pick one and unfurl it to reveal one of the following: *Corner office. Cubicle. CFO's office. CEO's office. Front desk.* And just like that, they have chosen their new digs for the next few months. Like, for realsies. The CFO has traded in a luxurious corner office for the administrative assistant's front desk, the CEO ends up in a cubicle, HR gets the CEO's office, and so on.

Sherry says that by giving people the chance to experience what the view looks like from where their colleagues sit on a daily basis—literally—these office swaps foster empathy, which in turn fosters more productive cooperation, communication, and connection. And, bonus points, it weeds out employees who put the *I* in *entitled.*

Productive Disruption

1. On small scraps of paper, write down the names or descriptions of all the offices, cubicles, or work spaces occupied by the people who report to you. Fold each one and place it in a hat (a mug, bucket, or other container is fine too).
2. Invite team members to pick one.
3. Whatever they pick becomes their new office for one week, one month, or even one year.
4. A few days after everyone has moved into their new work space, call a meeting to check in. This will likely spark a healthy discussion around hierarchy, teamwork, growth mindset, and weird stuff found in desk drawers.
5. If you need to do it on the D.L., try it as a thought experiment.

CHAPTER 3

TAKE PERMISSION—
'CAUSE NO ONE IS GONNA GIVE IT TO YOU

> Some friends of mine work in an office. They were getting really nervous from their coffee breaks, so they started to have wig breaks. They tried on wigs for fifteen minutes. They found this relaxing. So that's Wig Therapy.
>
> —LAURIE ANDERSON, *Performance Artist*

WHEN I WAS sixteen years old I applied for my first job at a place called Snow Oasis, which was neither snowy nor an oasis. It was a run-down shack in Arizona that sold shaved ice bathed in flavored syrups. The sugary "snow" was super fun to eat, but, as it turned out, not as much fun to serve.

I remember the interview process being surprisingly rigorous, considering that I was a teenager being hired to sell flavored ice. I sat on one side of a rickety picnic bench in the middle of a small asphalt parking lot with my soon-to-be boss, Allen, sitting on the other.

ALLEN: Why do you want to work here?
TANIA: I like the product.
ALLEN: What do you think you can bring to Snow Oasis?
TANIA: A sense of wonder.

ALLEN: How will you fit in your studies with your hours here?

TANIA: I don't study. Just kidding! I'm great at time management.

ALLEN: Would you be willing to commit to one year of employment?

TANIA: Totally.

Then Allen looked me in the eye with the intensity of a Major League baseball player winding up for the last pitch of a tie-breaking championship game and asked the million-dollar question.

ALLEN: So, TanYa . . . where do you see yourself five years from now?

TANIA: (*without missing a beat*) On *Saturday Night Live*!

ALLEN: (*rather flatly*) Oh.

Somehow, I got the job (lucky me), though in retrospect I'm pretty sure it's because he was desperate, not because I told him what he wanted to hear. I was supposed to say something like, "Well, Allen, for the next two to three years, I see myself shining in my current role, coming up with innovative new flavors like Cactus Snow and Snow Way You Can Resist This Strawberry. Then, in four years, I see myself starting my own Snow Oasis franchise, maybe in a slightly larger shack. In five years, I see myself attending the Shaved Snow Summit and receiving the Shaved Ice Ice Baby Achievement Award and thanking you, Allen, for being the best boss that anyone in the flavored ice business has ever had!"

Alas, this bright future as a snow cone tycoon was not to be mine. After being a faithful customer at Snow Oasis for a few years, gaining entrance into the shack had initially seemed like being invited to peek behind the curtain and see the great Wizard of Oz. But, just like the Wizard ends up being some schlumpy dude in a cheap suit, it wasn't long before the grandeur of Snow Oasis was revealed as an optical illusion too. By that I mean the tiny dirty shack actually turned out to be smaller and dirtier on the inside than it looked to be on the outside. Further adding to the enjoyment was the vague but persistent smell of meat, due to the meat-slicing machine that inexplicably inhabited that tiny shack. Yuck.

On my first day as a proud Snow Oasis employee, Allen showed me the tricks of the trade. Lift and pour a fifty-pound bag of foul-smelling powder into a comically large cauldron, add tons of water, and stir until every muscle in both arms ached and burned. Then, while Allen wheeled the snow cauldron into the freezer, I was to wrap a stained apron around the lower half of my body and engage with a surprisingly high number of customers lined up in front of the waist-high window.

As soon as I slid open the walk-up window, the unrelenting flurry of orders began. Mind you, this was before Square and Apple Pay and Bitcoin; back then we didn't even have fancy cash registers that did the heavy lifting. Which meant that you still had to count the change you gave back to customers, praying you did the math right so you wouldn't get any money docked from your already scrawny paycheck. This was also a time when running a credit card took a solid seven minutes, because you had to place it on what looked like a mini medieval torture device and then, with all your upper-body strength, aggressively push a stiff plastic bar across the length of the card in hopes that it would trace all sixteen digits . . . but more often than not it didn't, and then you'd have to do it again, only this time with the customer's angry glare boring a hole in your forehead.

It didn't take long for me to realize that operating archaic payment devices, scooping shaved ice into Styrofoam cups, and taking orders from sugar addicts were not in my skill set. Just four days into my tenure at Snow Oasis, I was already beginning to suffer from extreme claustrophobia as well as a general sensation of grossed-out-ness due to the proximity of the meat-slicing machine. So, I gave my one-hour notice, made myself a half-strawberry and half-lemon shaved ice for the road, and left that shit shack never to return again.

"Allen, listen," I told him. "I'm traveling quite a bit these days, so this isn't going to work for me. I'm leaving the Snow Oasis. Effective immediately."

Truth be told, most of the traveling I was doing as an under-employed, chubby teenager was to the corner store to purchase Little Debbie snack cakes. But nonetheless, my abrupt resignation from my crappy teenage job taught me a valuable lesson that I've been following ever since. Somehow, at sixteen years old, I had the huevos to clearly state, without any hesitation, "This isn't working for me" and "I'm leaving." I didn't ask anyone for permission to quit my job. I didn't blame anyone for my choice to work there in the first place. I didn't complain about the possible health code violations or the meat slicer. I made a decision that served me (and that almost certainly served the customers I undoubtedly shortchanged literally and figuratively), and that was that.

Why should any of us ask for permission to do anything in the service of our dreams, when we could simply *take* permission instead?

Can you imagine if the Wright brothers had waited around for permission? If Orville was all, "Wilbur, dude, will you ask Mom if it's cool if we fly this plane we just built?" And Wilbur was like, "Mom! Is it cool if Orville and I try to fly?" And Susan (their mom) was like, "Hells to the no! I already got TB, are you boys trying to kill me?! Now, keep your damn feet on the ground and come help me in the kitchen." Obviously, those two little Trespassers didn't wait around for someone to give them permission to take flight, they just took it. Someone will always give you a reason not to pursue your dreams if you ask them. So don't ask.

As kids, we instinctively knew that asking for permission was for suckers. If we wanted a Twinkie for lunch but all we had in our lunchbox was a plastic bag filled with miniature carrots, we didn't ask our teacher if we could trade our crappy snack with a good-natured classmate, we just did it! If we spotted a pile of cardboard boxes our neighbor left out on the curb on garbage day and wanted to turn them into a box fort in our garage, we didn't ask our parents for a building permit, we just built it! If we wanted to climb fences, trees, mountains, anything that stood still long enough for us to get a foothold on, we didn't ask if it was okay, we found a way to scale it. Taking permission is part of our DNA. I like to call it our Y-NOT chromosome.

So, Y-NOT try this out? What's one thing you're itching to do at work that nobody has given you permission to do? I'm not talking about encasing an office mate's stapler in Jell-O or printing out a company check to "cash," I'm talking about doing something that will reinvigorate not just you, but also your company, colleagues, and culture.

If you're scared of consequences, don't worry. As long as you are doing something productive, something creative, something that will bring value to your team or company (and it's not illegal), you can't get busted. You'll just be doing your job while inspiring more creativity, dignity, energy, joy, and respect for you and everyone involved.

For example, Y-NOT brainstorm all the problems that the

company isn't paying attention to right now? Is there one that, if addressed, could move your company's mission forward? Come up with three creative ways to solve it. Then present your ideas at the next all-hands meeting.

SOMEONE WILL ALWAYS GIVE YOU A REASON NOT TO PURSUE YOUR DREAMS IF YOU ASK THEM. SO DON'T ASK.

Or Y-NOT start an unauthorized Pizza and Perspective lunch series? Just pick a few people you'd like to get to know from other departments, write them an email, and invite them to lunch on you. You get to learn about another job, department, person, or perspective while eating pizza. What could be better? Maybe pizza and a cupcake. Well, guess what? You don't need permission for that cupcake either. Just take it!

So what will you take permission to do? Here are a few other ideas to get you started:

Productive Disruption

1. Send a group email to your team inviting them to a ten-minute dance party in your cubicle or office.
2. Spruce up a shared work space (lobby, break room, bathroom, floor, ceiling) with holiday decorations, inspiring quotes, flowers, art.
3. Dare to share your vision for the company . . . with the CEO.
4. Introduce yourself to someone in the company who does something you always wanted to learn about, and ask if you could shadow the person for a day or two.
5. Give your coworkers permission to take permission: Hand out stickers or slips of paper that read PERMISSION.

Need more motivation? Ask yourself:

Is this going to enliven a person, team, or idea?
Who is going to stop me from doing this?
What am I waiting for?

If you answered: "Yes," "No one," and "I have no idea," then it's time to give yourself permission—to take permission!

CREATE A JOB TITLE ON PURPOSE

A few years ago, my friend Vince, who is an architect, announced, "My job title sucks! I want something cool, something that reflects who I am, like the Imagineers at Disney." I thought about his job title outrage for a minute and then offered, "What about . . . erectioneer! Cuz, you know, you erect buildings, and then the -eer part from Disney, and, well . . ."

Okay, maybe the title wasn't fit to print, but it did make me think about how sucky it is to be stuck with a sucky job title. It's bad enough that we are born stuck; you know, in the birth canal and all. And once we make it out and start walking and talking, some condescending adult pats us on our little noggin and asks, "What do you want to be when you grow up?" What the hell kind of loaded question is that to ask a pint-size human?! Not to mention the fact that the second we come up with an answer—whether it's astronaut or teacher or master of the universe or whatever—we're basically stuck with it. Now it becomes the answer we give every cheek-pinching relative and regurgitate on every "what I want to be when I grow up" writing assignment, and, a decade or so later, the answer we serve up to every well-meaning career counselor and college admissions adviser. Even if we're able to avoid this trap, the implication is that there is only ONE thing we can do/be/kick ass at in our lifetime. And that sucks.

Then, we start a job and we're shoved into the tiniest confinement of them all: a two-by-three-and-a-half-inch one. It's called a business card. We are given a job title, get assigned to a department, and soon we're trapped in a miniature billboard advertising who we are and what we do, even though, ironically, the reality is that most formal job titles say very little about what we actually do at all ("Client Data and Management Information Specialist," "Inventory Analyst for Sales, Foraging, and Aquatics," "Assistant Regional Manager," "Assistant to the Regional Manager").

Listen up, Trespassers: We are more than our job titles.

When I started working in the technology industry, I didn't have a title, but that didn't stop well-meaning people at conferences and meetups constantly asking, "So . . . what do you do?"

I would respond by getting self-conscious, then a little defensive, then self-conscious again, all while mining my brain for a job title that was in the ballpark of accurate, while making me sound as impressive and important as possible.

Ah . . . I'm a spokesperson for software. Wait . . . I'm curating code. I got it, I'm disrupting technology with empathy! Hold up, I'm . . . I'm . . . Hey, isn't that the CEO over there? I think he's waving at you to come over . . .

WE ARE MORE
THAN
OUR JOB TITLES.

It wasn't until I was being introduced onstage at the Landmark Ventures CIO Summit, where I was about to speak in front of four hundred chief information officers, that I understood the power that had been bestowed upon me. The fact that I didn't have a title wasn't weird or embarrassing, it was awesome! It meant that I was free to make one up—on purpose.

What happened was that Anthony Juliano, the emcee and CTO of Landmark Ventures, had stood up and begun to introduce me, "Tania is a CIO . . ."

Oh, hell no! Chief information officer? Where the heck did he get that faulty data from? I was already in a state of panic, having heard the speaker before me talk extensively about AI, IA, and VR. Unless the audience was interested in hearing a talk on

TMIs, UTIs, or LOL, I was out SOL. I was there to give an inspirational talk about sneaking creativity into corporations, not give
my advice on information risk management. I hadn't even been
planning to share my usual quick fix for all technology problems:
turn it off, count to ten, then turn it back on again.

But before I had a chance to get up and run to the nearest
exit, Anthony continued with his introduction. "She is a chief
inspiration officer."

Whew. How about that? All that time, when people had asked
me the typical "What do you do?" I'd understood the question
as "What is your job title?"—the adult equivalent of asking me
what I wanted to be when I grew up. But now I understood the
question as "What is your purpose, and what do you contribute
to your company on a daily basis?"

The norm in most office cultures goes something like this:
Get hired, receive a title. Get promoted, receive a new title. And
so on. But here's the thing. We ALL have the power to transform
this norm and invent our own job title. Here's how:

Let's say you love solving problems and making people feel
welcomed and your responsibilities include facilitating communications and processing orders. Instead of front desk manager,
you might find out that you are the Curator of Communications,
CEO of Workflow, Dispatching Diva, or Fabulous Confabulator.

If you don't have the authority to change your title officially,
ask if you can simply add your new title to your existing one. And
if that doesn't fly, who's to stop you from ordering a box of business cards with your chosen-on-purpose job title emblazoned on
them?

You can also do this as a team-building exercise. Exchange
lists with colleagues and invent new job titles for each other.
Even if those new titles aren't fit to print, this kind of creative

thinking is a chance to find a deeper connection to who we are and what we do at work. And it gives us the power to expand our understanding of our work and approach it from a place of purpose, rather than as just a job.

Productive Disruption

1. Jot down all the stuff you love doing at work, the things that make you (and those around you) feel most alive.
2. Jot down the responsibilities of your position.
3. Come up with a job title that merges your purpose with your responsibilities.

DO ONE THING YOUR MOTHER SAID TO NEVER DO

Can you think of one thing—or two hundred—that your mother (or father or guardian) used to tell you to NEVER DO? I'm not talking about legit stuff like "don't push your little brother into oncoming traffic" or "never try to set your hair on fire." More like things that actually captured the spirit of experimentation but without any casualties. Things like:

1. *Don't ever become an artist/writer, you'll never make a living.*
2. *Never date a guy in a band.*
3. *Never leave the house without makeup.*
4. *Never leave dirty dishes in the sink overnight.*
5. *Don't ever, ever act like your father.*
6. *Don't even think about using the F word or I'll wash your*

mouth out with soap (on behalf of those of us who were coparented by Palmolive—fuck YOU, Palmolive!).

7. *And for the love of God, don't EVER let people know that you are happy (it just comes across as arrogant)!*

Now I want you to choose a couple of things from your list and take permission to DO THEM.

CHAPTER 4

LET YOUR
FREAK FLAG FLY

Don't worry about cool, make your own uncool.

—SOL LEWITT, *Conceptual Artist*

WHEN I WAS six years old and starting the first grade, I rode the school bus for the first time. I wanted to walk. I loved walking. But apparently it wasn't kosher for a parent to let a six-year-old walk six miles to and from school by herself. So, on orders from my mother, I lined up behind the other Trapper Keeper–carrying kids waiting for the big black-and-yellow bus to bounce up to our decrepit apartment complex and take us far, far away.

It being the first day of school and all, I was decked out in my finest pink-and-white-striped T-shirt "dress" (I say "dress" because when looking back at photos of myself from this time, it's startlingly clear that I was in fact wearing a long T-shirt that my mother had tricked me into believing was a dress). My long brown hair was scooped up into two tight pigtails, and I was rocking my signature eyeglasses: dark brown plastic ovals that ate up most of my face thanks to the thick lenses required to correct my astigmatism. I had worn eyeglasses since I was four years old. And even though they didn't *look* cool, I *felt* cool in my glasses; they made me feel older, more intellectual, highly sophisticated, and totally unique because no one else my age wore them. Plus, my mom was always telling me how cute I looked in them.

The school bus snorted to a stop, I hugged my mother good-bye, and with a loud puff of air (not unlike the one they blast into your retina during an eye exam) the bus door popped open and I climbed aboard. There wasn't much time to find a seat, so I slid into a random pleather covered bench next to another little girl who looked to be my age. As the bus jerked forward, my seatmate turned to face me, leaned forward, and looked me square in the eye. I liked her assertiveness, that is, until she uttered the words that strike terror in every bespectacled first grader's heart: "Four eyes!" And every day, for the rest of the week, when I got on the school bus, that little menace managed to worm herself into a nearby seat and, with a diabolical gleam in her two eyes, call me "Four eyes!" Finally, I told my mom what was going on, not to tattle, of course, but because I needed some backup, some sage advice. Mom said, "You tell her that four eyes are better than two." Mom's observation was pure genius! What an idiot that little brat was; she sucked at math and at life.

So, the next day, I climbed on the bus and waited for the mini tyrant to sling her nasty slurs at me. Sure enough, that two-eyed twerp came slinking up next to me and let me have it. Only this time, instead of suppressing tears, I confidently spit back, "Four are better than two!" (And if I had known the word *booyah* at the time, I would have said that too.) And you know what she said? She said, "No, they're not." To which I . . . had no comeback.

Eventually I realized that my mathematically challenged seatmate was nothing but a bully in cute little-girl clothing who had figured out a way to fabricate a world in which she was awesome, and if she deemed you different or inferior, it was her God-given duty to make your life miserable. I was a freak, as she made quite clear, in her own snot-nosed six-year-old way, and if I wanted to be "cool," I'd have to lose the coke-bottle glasses and play by the rules that non–vision-impaired society had devised.

Where is that little girl today? Well, I have no idea, but she ain't one of the founders of Warby Parker or the creator of Google Glass, I'll tell you that much! Point is, we all know plenty of bullies just like her, masquerading as bosses, colleagues, frenemies, and even our own internal monologues, quick to point out our flaws and imperfections in hopes of shaming the originality right out of us. These child tyrants desperately want to keep us swaddled in the warm, safe cocoon of conformity. But though it may be tempting to cave to their wishes (after all, it's cozy in there) the truth is this: It's only when we dare to embrace our flaws and let our freak flags fly that we leave the cocoon and become stunning butterflies.

A few months ago, I was at a café getting my morning cappuccino. The barista was wearing a bright-yellow T-shirt with bold black letters stretched across the front that read GIRL POWER. After a few minutes, the kindred-spirit barista approached my table and gingerly set the full cappuccino down in front of me. Then she gestured toward it and said, "I'm sorry about the design." I looked down expecting to find just the café's signature leaf pattern etched into the layer of foam floating on top. Instead I saw an explosion of frothy, milky dots, several of which were literally morphing into beautiful heart shapes and stars before my eyes. It was magnificent, like nothing I'd ever seen. I asked her, "Why are you apologizing?" She looked down sheepishly and said, "I messed it up. All those dots shouldn't be there." I assured her that I loved it. "This is the most unique coffee design I've ever seen!" I insisted. Yet, she kept apologizing.

"Embrace your beautiful mistake," I told her. "In the sea of same, your design stands out."

And I meant it. In the thousands of cappuccinos I've consumed in my lifetime, I don't remember a single foam design but hers. Instead of flaws, I saw beauty.

That's the exact mindset you need as a Creative Trespasser.

EMBRACE YOUR BEAUTIFUL MISTAKES.

In the sixties, Eva Hesse was an up-and-coming artist pushing the boundaries between drawing, painting, and sculpting. She had moved from New York to Germany, leaving her art community and her good friend and fellow artist Sol LeWitt far behind. As she began experimenting with materials and ideas in her new studio, she became disillusioned by the art she was making; it didn't look quite like anyone else's. She started to question whether or not it was even art, whether or not she was even an artist, and soon her self-doubt became so consuming, she was ready to give up her passion altogether. When she described her woes in a letter to her buddy Sol, he responded with a powerful pep talk (in the form of a handwritten letter) inspiring her to lean into her imperfections and forge ahead with the innovative art she was making. He told her: "Don't worry about cool, make your own uncool. Make your own world. If you fear, make it work for you."

Here are some ways we can start to celebrate the stuff that makes us stand out and "make our own world," in anything we do.

CLAIM YOUR NONCONFORMITY
AT THE DOOR

Standing out can be a quiet gesture; it can be subtle, thoughtful, empathic. But it can also be loud, ruckus-filled, disruptive, or a combination of all of these. It can be standing onstage acting your heart out, or it can be working the equipment behind the curtain to make sure the set doesn't come crashing down.

It's time to stop apologizing for your flaws and start seeing the beauty in standing out. The next time you make an exquisite mistake—doodle an elaborate scene on your performance review form, answer the phone with "Hi, sexy," (forgetting that you gave your cell number to your most important customer) or misread the new Friday dress code guidelines and show up in a cropped top rather than cropped pants—instead of letting out a deflated "I'm so sorry," try saying, "I'm so unique!" Instead of checking your nonconformity at the door, claim it.

HUG YOUR INNER CHILD TYRANT

Let's face it, we all have a lil' goody-two-shoes (or two eyes) inside of us, a little part of ourselves that longs to fit in, insists that change is bad, and kicks our asses if we get out of line. It's time to show a little compassion for that little bully who has run a tight ship all these years and kept us from letting our freak flag fly. Even though she comes from a place of fear and anger and says annoying stuff like "If you don't play by the rules you're going to get fired," that pocket-sized buzzkill has probably saved our jobs, lives, and dreams more than once. So imagine hugging that surly little nugget. Tighter. Until she loosens up a bit. Until she cracks a smile. Then go back to giving that little goody-two-shoes a hard time.

PUT THE *I'M* IN (*I'M*)PERFECT

Close your eyes and picture all of your wonderful flaws, all the stuff that makes you uniquely, awkwardly YOU. Now picture each one of these unique qualities being taken away from you. The way you show up at work (and most dates) with your shirt inside out. How you harbor an unhealthy obsession for the Muppets. Literally salivating when a plate of French fries is within a ten-mile radius. Judging yourself for salivating. Judging yourself for being judgmental. Your untamable instinct to scream whenever you see a bug. The way you tear up when looking at puppy pictures. Your encyclopedic knowledge of fast-food restaurants. What are you left with? To be perfect is to be invisible. Try saying out loud: (*I'm*)perfect . . . *and so are you!*

TRY TO DO SOME *BAD* WORK

The more we spin our wheels trying to conform, the more invisible our creativity becomes. In his letter to Hesse, LeWitt also encouraged her to do BAD work—"the worst you can think of"—because he wanted to show her that perfection kills creativity. "You must practice being stupid, dumb, unthinking, empty," he told her.

So today, try letting go of the need to do GOOD work. Let go of making things exactly the way other people make them or doing things the way other people do them. "Mainly relax," as LeWitt put it, "and let everything go to hell."

Within the scope of the work that you do, is there something you've never tried before? Something you aren't talented or proficient in? Something that you might even suck at doing? DO it! Look, if the finished product sucks, no big whoop. You're not required to turn in your sucky work to your boss or client. This is about opening up new channels for thinking and expression that will elevate the work you eventually *do* show others.

As my friend Coco Brown, CEO of the Athena Alliance, told me, "Conformity at best will perfect something that already exists. If you want something groundbreaking, you have to be willing to think and act differently, to test, and to take respectful risks. It's what everyone who does something amazing does."

LOSE YOURSELF IN THE FREEDOM OF MAKING SOMETHING MESSY, OF LETTING EVERYTHING GO TO HELL.

CHAPTER 5

SUSPEND DISBELIEF

When you change the way you look at things,
the things you look at change.

—MAX PLANCK, *Theoretical Physicist*

I STEPPED OVER the edge and felt the ground beneath me slip away. There was no net, just sheer adrenaline and then . . . clear blue sky. No, I didn't jump out of an airplane (I puke *in* airplanes, so jumping out of 'em . . . forget it!). I jumped into a totally new profession at forty-two years old, and while I was still in midair, friends and family demanded to know, "Why are you leaving a great job to go into an industry you know NOTHING about?" "Are you nuts?" "WHAT THE #*%! ARE YOU DOING?!" To which I responded, *I don't know! Maybe! HELP!*

Then, mercifully, my parachute deployed, and the force of gravity pulled me down to solid ground.

This is how I fell into the tech industry. But the scary part wasn't the jumping. That part was fun—it was the landing that got me.

The idea of jumping into the unknown is one of the foundational concepts in theater, where it's called *suspension of disbelief.* Poet and philosopher Samuel Taylor Coleridge came up with this term in the early 1800s to describe how, when we gather in a creative space, like a theater, we agree collectively to let go of everything we know to be true about the world around us; we suspend all of our assumptions and perceptions and take a poetic leap of faith into an unknown world together.

For me, it all started with that unexpected call from the afore-mentioned hip company Axosoft. "We'd love to talk with you about software." At first, I thought they must have had the wrong number, or been a telemarketer, except for the fact that I knew so little about software, not even a telemarketer would want to talk to me about it. When I say I knew nothing about software, I mean NOTH-ING. I'm not joking. At that point in my career, I thought Linux was a character in the *Peanuts* comic strip and digital whiteboarding was a torture technique, and all the term AI brought to mind was a British person asking for more beer in a pub: *'Ay! I want another pint!*

Regardless, as an enthusiastically curious person, I took the meeting anyway. I knew Axosoft was a cool company because I had given a talk about infusing creativity into the workplace at their offices a year prior, and when given a tour, I had spotted magical wonders the likes of which I had never seen in a place of business: cabinets with snacks spilling out of them, a workout room (probably due to the aforementioned snacks), open ergo-nomic workstations, and people playing video games . . . during the workday! Between the unlimited supply of granola bars and the colorful, playful work spaces, Axosoft felt like a summer camp for adults. Plus, all the employees (who were seated in beanbag chairs during the talk and dressed as if every day was Casual Fri-day) had been totally engaged and asked really great questions.

The CEO of Axosoft, Lawdan Shojaee, who is a petite, high-energy firecracker of a human being, greeted me at the front door and whisked me into an "all-purpose room" (that's what cool companies call a conference room). With one eye on me and the other on the text message she was typing furiously, she said, "We really like your energy, that's why we brought you in!" "I really like *your* energy," I replied. "That's why I came in." "But we're not offering you a job," she informed me, to which I replied, while simultaneously wondering what the heck I was doing there, "I don't need a job."

That's when she looked up from her phone and said, "But we've always wanted to have an evangelist. You'd make a great evangelist." I processed this information for a moment. Then I turned to her and said, "That would totally freak my Jewish mom out. YES, I want to evangelize with you!"

I quickly found out, much to my dismay, that an evangelist in the tech world is not a religious zealot at all. A tech evangelist is someone who is fanatically committed to a company's products and goes out into the world preaching the good word of this higher power in order to woo new customers into paying for the elation and transcendence that a great software product can provide. So, totally different. Except kind of the same.

We decided to take a leap of faith together. We wanted to see what was possible when we let go of the idea that in order to contribute to an industry, one needed to already be proficient in its products and processes. *Gulp.*

As it turned out, Lawdan was an outsider on the inside, just like I was. In fact, she had recently taken the reins from her husband as CEO of the company, and as a trained pilot with a PhD in physical therapy, she too was an unlikely fit for the position.

So, even though it wasn't her intention to offer me a job that day, she understood the benefits of entering a space with fewer preconceived ideas and a fresh, outsider perspective. One amazing quality about Lawdan (as I would learn later) is that she implicitly trusted and followed her gut—her "second brain," as she called it.

So, that's how I landed behind a desk (more like an open workstation with three large monitors dividing my "office" from the one next to mine), trying to learn as much as I could about this unknown world of software. "So . . ." I asked Lawdan. "What is our supercool software, anyway?!" Was it an app? An email system? Was it a Word-like platform for writing stuff? Ooh!! She said, "It's an Agile project management software, for software developers. You know, SaaS, B2B."

No. I did not know. It was as if I was in the audience of a game show and one of the real contestants had dropped out so they grabbed me, threw me up onstage, and smacked me in the pie hole with a spotlight! *SaaS? Uh . . . What is "Things my little sister has"? B2B? I got this one!! What is "Bedrooms we convert into charming hotels"?*

Clearly, I had some catching up to do, so for the next two months, I took a crash course in the company's software and the methodology behind making it. One thing I discovered was that the developers at Axosoft used something called Agile methodology, which is based on collaboration (insights and input by different departments), feedback (having people test the software and make suggestions), and iteration (tweaking the software, based on feedback) before releasing it (offering it to an intended audience). *Holy smokes!* I thought. *That's pretty much the same process by which we create theater.* Collaboration (playwright, actors, set designer, and others offering insights and adding layers), feedback (utilizing rehearsals and performances to gauge audience responses: did they laugh at jokes, tear up, leave, etc.), and iterations (new drafts of the script based on feedback), and then putting it out into the world (opening night, baby!).

The realization that the creative process looks much the same, whether we're making software or theater, was what ultimately cushioned my landing into this strange new world. And three months into my job, just as I was really getting my sass on, I leapt right out of my comfort zone again. What happened was, Lawdan came to my colleague Sara Breeding and me and told us that Axosoft was sponsoring a big women in technology conference. She wanted to show up in a big way, so could Sara and I please "come up with a 'BIG' idea"?

So, Sara and I started brainstorming and came up with . . . nothing. And then more nothing. At this point, I decided to go for a walk in the hopes it would help me get unstuck. As I walked, I thought about the task at hand, about women in technology, about women in the tech space, about women in *many* spaces, and how oftentimes, women aren't seen, heard, or celebrated for the superheroes we are.

I thought about my own experience as an outsider in the tech world and the unexpected parallels I had found between theater and Agile methodology. And then I wondered: what if we could take the theater's principle of suspending disbelief and apply it to women in technology? What if we could let go of all the assumptions and unwritten rules of the actual world and leap into a world where women are paid as much as their male counterparts? What if we could jump into a place where women make up 50 percent of C-suite positions? And what if we could land in a school where half the twelve-year-olds taking a coding class are girls? And what if one of those girls is there because she sees herself in the female teacher? Because she sees herself in the girl sitting next to her. Because she *sees herself.* And in herself she sees a superhero.

Then I saw an image in my mind's eye. The women's bathroom symbol. You know her, she wears a triangle dress, has a circle for a head, and is usually found hanging out on public restroom doors around the world. I knew this symbol was instantly recognizable across cultures and genders, and I knew in my "second brain" that it had to be the creative breakthrough we had been looking for.

I went back to the office and shared this glimmer of an idea with Sara, and the two of us started spitballing in hopes of a "big idea" emerging. Then something got stuck in my craw. The shape of her dress, that iconic triangle. It looked like a dress, but it also kinda looked like a . . . cape! The more I thought about it, the more I convinced myself that bathroom lady was, in fact, wearing a cape. And before considering how weird that sounded, I enthusiastically announced to Sara, "I think she's wearing a cape!" Sara nodded kindly, like one might nod when an aging parent asks, "Have you ever heard about the time I . . . ?" and then proceeds to tell the same story they've told you a hundred times.

I ran over to my computer, printed out the ubiquitous women's bathroom symbol, and with a pencil (and a prayer) drew a few lines to reveal that she was, in fact, wearing a cape. Then I showed her to Sara, who excitedly proclaimed, "It was never a dress!"

Only after we suspended disbelief and checked our preconceived assumptions at the door were we able to see it: *This symbol that we've walked past a million times without blinking an eye, something we only really ever notice when, you know, we gotta go, was actually a superhero this whole time!* We were just looking at her the wrong way.

We took the idea to the boss, and she shared it with the team, whose reactions ranged from "This is the worst idea EVER," to "This is awesome," and everything in between. Eventually Lawdan gave her blessing, then we quickly enlisted our graphic designer and got to work on making #ItWasNeverADress into reality.

We launched the #ItWasNeverADress campaign in April 2015 at the Girls in Tech Catalyst Conference in Phoenix, Arizona. A launch sounds big and fancy, but really, all we did was set up a small booth and hand out stickers featuring our caped superhero. Then I gave a talk about the campaign's goal to shift perceptions and assumptions about women in technology and beyond.

Here's where things took an unexpected turn. Someone at the conference posted an image of the sticker on Twitter and Facebook and wrote, "Cannot unsee." Within twenty-four hours, there were 18 million organic impressions across the web—which is tech talk for millions of people liking, retweeting, sharing, and championing our message. Within three days, just about every major media outlet in the entire world had picked up the story: CNN, *Time*, the *Huffington Post*, the *India Times*, Mashable, Bored Panda, Yahoo New Zealand, the *New York Times*, and a ton more.

Within a few weeks, companies of all stripes were taking the reimagined image and tweaking it to sell their wares. But rather than calling in the lawyers and trying to stop all these people from coopting our creation, we decided to embrace them. After all, as a relatively small, Agile software company, we were in the business of selling collaboration tools, and our goal here was to start, not dominate or commodify, a conversation. So rather than worry about the fact that our brainchild was being used to sell feminine hygiene products and knockoff tees, we set up an #ItWasNeverADress website to serve as a community-curated space. A space for people to share their stories, download free posters and images of the bathroom lady that could be customized, and more.

All for the purpose of encouraging people to come up with their own creative possibilities beyond the cape, which they did, and shared, and soon the internet was teeming with bathroom ladies in judges' robes, lab coats, caps and gowns, and more.

Then we got on the horn with Arizona State University and set up a need-based STEAM scholarship for students working across disciplines.

What we created at Axosoft, as a team, sparked a global conversation that is still going strong today. People shared personal stories on the website with titles like "Refusing to be Silent." Men wrote about how the campaign helped them see that their team lacked the kind of gender diversity that fosters innovation and have made it their mission to hire more women. Many celebrities shared the image online, including Alanis Morissette, Uzo Aduba, Elizabeth Gilbert, and—appropriately—*both* Wonder Women: Lynda Carter and Gal Gadot.

The message helped millions of girls and women let go of preconceived notions and start to see superheroes in different forms all around them, even within them. And by superhero, I'm not talking about someone with the power to slay dragons, or outrun a locomotive, or leap buildings in a single bound. I'm not talking about the movie or comic book character who swoops in and saves the day; I'm talking about superheroes of the *everyday*. After all, *super* means above and beyond, and *hero* means to act with courage, so being a superhero of the everyday simply means knowing that each one of us possesses the power to go above and beyond: to boldly stretch the limits of what is possible, every day.

That's the power of suspending disbelief, and it's one that you too can tap to ignite your own creative spark.

Look, if I could jump out of a metaphorical airplane and land on solid ground, anyone can—including you. Here are some exercises to help you feel a little more confident suspending disbelief, leaping into new arenas, and seeing the many creative possibilities in the world around you.

FIND YOUR INNER T

The concept of T-shaped skills is a big deal in Agile software development and in other industries too, cuz they encourage us to leap into more collaborations with more creativity and gusto. The idea is that we all possess a depth of knowledge in one or two areas (the vertical bar of a T) and some broader skills that allow us to collaborate across disciplines (the horizontal bar of a T). When we invite depth and breadth to our collaborations, our creativity grows exponentially.

To locate your inner T, you can start by tackling a problem at work that everyone is looking to solve. Identify the areas where your knowledge runs deep, and invite people with different skills to the table. Agree to suspend disbelief, and brainstorm a list of the most unbelievable, outlandish solutions. *Like, what if we had a competitive game show where we invited our competitors to face off with us in activities associated with our industry, in front of a live audience, with our customers as judges? What if we reached out to dissatisfied customers and offered them something wacky and memorable? What if we looked for new talent in new places? What if we launched a brand campaign in outer space? What if . . .*

Remember, in order to suspend disbelief, you have to believe that anything is possible. And it's much easier to see all the possibilities when people with diverse skills, expertise, and backgrounds come together. When there's more diversity in problem solving, there's less likely to be one "truth," or one agreed-upon set of rules, preconceptions, and assumptions, and more likely to be unbelievable, outlandish, and innovative solutions that actually address pressing problems. So let's ask ourselves one more "what if": What if you start finding your inner T today?

LEAVE LIMITS BEHIND

Ever muster up the courage to take a leap of faith and then, while in midair, hear people yelling, "What do you think you're doing?? Are you crazy??" Or, even worse, ever yelled it yourself? "I totally suck. I'm not qualified. I don't have the skills. I'm not even creative. I can't come up with a single inspiring idea! There's nothing I can do about it; I'm just that kind of person."

We've all performed an inner monologue like this inside our own head at one time or another. But each time we do, we are cementing these self-defeating beliefs in our head, making it that much harder to break free of them.

Limiting beliefs are the number one silent killer of creativity, more deadly than flying cockroaches, giving a speech to a crowd of thousands in your underwear (you know, the ones with the disintegrating elastic band), or running into your boss on a Saturday while high. When we cling to the belief that how things are is how they always will be, we get trapped in a mental prison of our own making. But when we believe that logic and limits are subject to change, then the world is full of possibilities.

The ability to suspend disbelief is a skill. And just like any other skill, it takes repeated practice before you are able to do it well. Here's a simple exercise:

Productive Disruption

1. Today, when you go into work, find an object or symbol you have somehow overlooked, something you pass every day.

2. See it. See it in the context of and in contrast to the things surrounding it.

3. Turn it upside down, inside out, flip it around, shake it, and spin it on its head until you see it in a new way.

4. Remember, we're only limited by *how* we see, not what we are looking at.

DEFY GRAVITY

For those of you who don't know Elizabeth Streb, she is a dancer, choreographer, MacArthur "Genius" Fellow, and creator of an entirely new way of moving called PopAction, which fuses dance, gymnastics, circus, and extreme sports together. Streb says things like "Anything that is too safe is not an action." And "Go to the edge and peer over it. Be willing to get hurt, but not so hurt that you can't come back again." Instead of pursuing a traditional career as a choreographer, Streb knew that her calling lay in testing the limits of physics by using her training in choreography to explore the age-old question: Can we fall *up*?

Of course, I didn't know any of this until *after* I ended up taking a one-day intensive dance class with Streb, thanks to a friend who said, "Hey, there's a free movement class open to the public, wanna go?"

Turns out, it was a master class for real dancers, not curious civilians with two left feet and a low threshold for pain, but by the time I found this out, I was lying flat on my stomach, alongside twenty real dancers, trying to figure out what the heck Streb meant by her instruction to "jump up."

I soon found out, as my decidedly more sprightly classmates began popping up into the air like shimmering fish leaping out of the ocean to catch a glimpse of the sun after a cold winter, while I could muster the strength only to lift one arm up off the mat, making me look more like a chicken with a broken wing than a silver fish dancing in the air. And this was just the warm-up. By the end of the class, I had not managed to defy gravity, but I had certainly reaffirmed its existence. Repeatedly.

Somehow, though, I made it to the end. I pushed myself to the edge, looked over and thought, "OUCH," and kept pushing anyway.

It eventually dawned on me that this painful exercise had actually been an act of Creative Trespassing in disguise. For Streb, I later learned, defying gravity is a way of questioning long-held assumptions about the world, a way of pushing up against systems, and of merging divergent skills to find a new way to fly. As it turns out, when math, gravity, and choreography collide, it *is* possible to fall up.

You can defy gravity too, in your own, less physically demanding way. *Anyone* can cultivate curiosity, push up against limits and systems, merge his or her skills, and learn to fly. What assumptions about the world will you challenge to "fall up"?

WHEN WE BELIEVE THAT LOGIC AND LIMITS ARE SUBJECT TO CHANGE, THEN THE WORLD IS FULL OF POSSIBILITIES.

My buddy Jessie Shternshus is the founder of The Improv Effect, a company that uses improv to empower people to become better listeners, collaborators, and problem solvers. She believes that practicing improv—which forces you to invent characters, situations, and stories without any pre-established rules or instructions—helps people get in the habit of checking their assumptions at the door and asking "what if" so they can see new perspectives and possibilities in their work. Here's a Productive Disruption she shared with me.

Productive Disruption

1. Think of a place you spend time in on a regular basis: your home, the train, your office.
2. Write down all the things you typically find in that space. In an office, for example, that would likely include desks, staplers, computers, chairs, whiteboards, paperclips, shitty coffee, etc.
3. Eliminate one item and ask yourself: What if an office didn't have desks? Could it still be a functioning office? What could take its place?
4. Eliminate one more item, then another, until you are able to imagine an entirely new type of office.
5. Next time you are faced with a sticky problem, try using this method to eliminate assumptions and make room for more dynamic solutions.

CHAPTER 6

DITCH
SCHOOL

Innovation is made possible by the width and
breadth of a person's rummaging around the
world.

—ANNE BOGART, *Theater Director*

DID YOU EVER ditch school as a kid or teenager? Come on, you can tell me, you're talking to a professional school ditcher right here! Remember the mix of exhilaration and fear, the intense focus it took to make a clean getaway? The imagination it took to come up with barely believable excuses when you got busted and called to the principal's office? *I don't know WHY, my mom just said it was urgent, so . . . One of my relatives got into a boating accident. I know we're in a landlocked state, that's what makes it so scary!* And the age-old favorite (particularly effective with male teachers and principals): *I got my period.* For me, ditching school was the ultimate training ground for becoming a Creative Trespasser.

Remember the adventures you had? Huddling behind the Micky D's eating French fries with your best friend and comparing notes about sex (before you ever had it)? Sharing urban legends about the creepy boarded-up old house near your school? Sneaking into any building that didn't have a guard and riding the elevator up and down a million times? Sneaking into an R-rated movie even though you were only thirteen? Walking miles through strange neighborhoods and getting so lost in conversation that you just barely made it home by dinnertime? Doing at least one thing you were definitely NOT supposed to do?

Remember what you learned? So many life skills they didn't teach you in school, like how to inhale a cigarette. How to bullshit authority figures. How to get your mitts on books you actually wanted to read. Do you remember that feeling? The energy, the curiosity, the sense of being truly alive? Well, we're gonna reclaim it, starting now.

That's right, I'm telling you to ditch work. Now, look, I don't want you to lose your job, so do what you gotta do and use your lunch break or take a sick day, a vacation day, a mental health day (personally I think all companies should offer "ditch days"). Then, during your lunch break, when everyone else is slumped over their desks eating soggy salad or sitting around a too-small cafeteria table making polite conversation over microwaved macaroni and cheese, you and a colleague are gonna bolt! Go to a library or museum, walk through a new park or neighborhood, learn how to inhale the fresh air outside your cubicle. Today you are going to learn something from the outside and then bring it into your work. Ditch your cell phone, tablet, smartwatch. Today you're gonna disconnect in order to reconnect with your unruly, rebellious, teenage spark.

Hey, I wouldn't encourage you to do this unless I did it myself, all the time (so, booyah, Principal Brookes!). And being the delinquent that I am, I can personally attest to the fact that ditching work allows you to stumble on so many new people, perspectives, and possibilities that you never would have encountered inside the four walls of your office. It's how I've been able to meet great musicians, storytellers, and creators—usually posing as baristas—and offer them contracts; it's how I've been able to crowdsource marketing campaigns simply by walking through parks and chatting with people; it's how I've found big ideas hidden in the stacks of public libraries, on sidewalks, in parking lots.

It's so freeing to be outside and wandering during a workday that it almost feels subversive, like it's just a matter of time before a truant officer asks you why you're not at work and then busts you. But in reality it's most likely that the only person you're gonna get busted by is you. Think about it: Is there really anyone at work telling you that you can't leave the office and explore the world around you during your breaks, or take a personal day to go to a museum or the movies, or actually use the vacation time you have coming to you, even if it's just to sit at home watching all the classic films you've never seen or reading a book?

Oh, sure, there will always be those people shooting disapproving looks or even commenting on your deigning to take breaks during the workday (despite the mountains of research showing that employees who do are more productive and creative and get better results over the long term). I once had a boss who would try to shame me whenever I'd leave for my break, "OH, leaving for lunch again, huh?" At that job NO ONE left the building for lunch. Like, ever. And it sucked.

Of course, that's what made me even more determined to leave during my lunch breaks, to get some fresh air and perspective. Sometimes I went to grab a coffee or a bite to eat; other times I just walked aimlessly or to let a problem or project I was tackling simmer. At first, I worried that my boss thought I was lazy or that I didn't give a crap about my work. Then I realized: He was jealous! And apparently other people around the office were too, because pretty soon coworkers were sidling up to me and, in hushed tones, asking, "Where do you *go* during lunch?" I'd tell them and invite them to join me anytime they wanted to. Soon, one or two people were coming with me, then a few, and, after a while, lots of people were leaving for lunch . . . on their own.

The simple act of leaving during a lunch break was enough to spark our imaginations and give us a boost of inspiration that translated directly into our work. Even though we were just walking, breathing fresh air, and informally brainstorming, it felt like playing hooky, like we didn't have to wait until Saturday to play, to explore, to get our creative juices flowing.

Getting out into the world and wandering with no agenda is a surefire plan for finding your spark. Once you do, you'll be able to ignite innovations with more fire and passion than you ever thought possible.

GO OUT FOR A SPIN

Elizabeth Cutler, cofounder of SoulCycle and fellow Creative Trespasser, is a total truant! But far from hurting her career, ditching is what has made her so freaking successful in the first place. First she ditched the typical fitness routines because she said "they felt like work" and instead set out to create a workout "that felt more human and free . . . something as efficient as it is joyful." So, she joined forces with cofounder Julie Rice, and together they spun their inspiration into a brand of gold.

As you can imagine, creating (and running) a company that is disrupting the fitness world can require an exorbitant number of hours stuck at a desk. So, Elizabeth ditched her desk too! She began taking a creative day each week; one full day where she gets up from her desk, ditches the demands of running a business, and does something that isn't directly related to her job. As she puts it: "I leave my desk and listen for the things that call to me and then I answer the call. I walk and explore different neighborhoods, wander the streets, and reconnect with my creative self."

> **Productive Disruption**
>
> **1.** Claim one day, one hour, even ten minutes, every week, as your creative time.
> **2.** Ditch your desk.
> **3.** Wander.
> **4.** Reconnect with your creative self.

DISCONNECT AND DISCOVER SOMETHING NEW

I recently spoke with the artist (and professor of art) Angela Ellsworth, who was generous enough to share an exercise that she gives her art students on the first day of class.

Be forewarned: This exercise has made some of the coolest-cucumber art students whine like petulant toddlers, moan and groan like pissed-off teenagers, and, in some cases, experience total hysterical meltdowns. It's that powerful.

On the first day of class Ellsworth asks all of the students to ditch their devices. All iPads, smartphones, and computers are to be placed on a large round table in the middle of the room. She asks the students to place their purses, backpacks, and messenger bags on said table as well.

She then instructs the students to leave their belongings in the classroom and go outside—get off campus, walk around town, go wherever they are drawn to wander—for exactly ninety minutes. They have to meander alone, not as a group, and the only thing they can carry with them is a bottle of water.

As soon as these instructions are given, without fail, the students totally panic. And, each semester, the same anxiety-induced questions come out of their mouths:

"How will we know what time it is?" To which, Ellsworth replies, "Ask someone."

"What if I get lost?" Ellsworth shoots back, "Pay attention to your surroundings."

"What if we go outside without our phones and get hurt? Get hit by a car? Pass out? How will anyone know what has become of us?!" At which point, Ellsworth usually explains how there was a time, not so long ago, when none of us had cell phones and, somehow, we are all still alive.

One year a student went nuclear, suggesting that the entire assignment was "a very dangerous liability issue!"

Yet Ellsworth always persists and sends them off: fully clothed, but technologically nude. And somehow, every semester, all of the students make it back to the classroom on time, unscathed and totally transformed.

Then there's the post-exercise discussion, where students share their experience with this experiment. Year after year, they recount how simply wandering, without a set destination, blew their minds open. Once, a student talked about a parking structure that he had previously seen as nothing more than an annoying obstacle forcing him to take a detour to class, but that day he discovered that if you climbed to the top, you got a breathtaking view of the entire city. When the heat of the late-summer sun forced her to look for shade, another student found a tree she walked by every day and had never noticed before. Instead of feeling anxious without their mobile devices, most of the students expressed feeling a sense of relief. One student said, "That was the most freedom I've experienced since I was a little kid."

Contrary to what students believe before they engage in the assignment, Ellsworth's intention isn't to torture them, it's to force them to explore; to see the places they encounter every single day in a new way, unencumbered by texting, talking, or rushing to get somewhere. It's an opportunity to discover the magic in the familiar.

We spend so much of our lives trying to get from A to B that we miss the space in between, the space that invites us to be present in the moment, to find the shade, to climb up to the top of a structure and look out onto the horizon. Only when we ditch our devices, ditch our busy schedules, ditch our need for a purpose, a goal, a destination, do we discover something new and beautiful about the world around us.

WALK OFF THE JOB

People always ask me, "Do you ever get a creative block?" to which I always respond, "No." Sure, I get snagged while trying to come up with creative ideas (all the time), but whenever I'm feeling stuck, I have a nearly foolproof strategy: I ditch whatever I'm working on and go for a walk. Walking helps me to disconnect from my computer in order to reconnect with the world around me; there's no autocorrecting a misstep; every step is correct. Walking makes me feel totally free and completely alive. It reminds me that we coexist with architecture, nature, sounds, and beings. Every step is full of life. Whenever I find myself stuck in a chair, mindset, or pattern, I get my ass up and put my walking shoes on. Even if it's only for ten minutes, being outside and in motion inspires me to see things from a new perspective.

Turns out I'm not alone. We all know those now iconic walking meetings that Steve Jobs used to take to encourage creative thinking. Well, it turns out that just a few minutes of strolling is potent enough to bust through the heartiest of creative blocks. Believe it or not, when researchers at Stanford conducted a study on the impact walking has on creativity, they found that walking improved a person's creative output by as much as 60 percent.

So, when you're feeling like you've explored all the possible solutions to a problem and still can't solve it . . . walk off the job! Even if it's just for ten, fifteen, or twenty minutes, and even if you don't have a "eureka" moment right then, it will help open up your mind and senses and break you out of your rut. Then come back and get to your creative work.

CHAPTER 7

THINK
INSIDE THE BOX

Never be limited by other people's limited
imaginations.

—DR. MAE JEMISON, *Astronaut and Dancer*

ON MY FIRST DAY as a member of a large corporately structured
organization, I showed up wearing an orange blazer, blue sneakers, black Buddy Holly eyeglasses, and my finest vintage T-shirt;
if my new job had been lead singer of a nerdcore band, I would
have totally rocked the look. So it was really unfortunate that I
had been hired by the Scottsdale Museum of Contemporary Art
and not Nerdapalooza.

I feel it's important to reveal here that I'm probably the least
likely person to ever work for an art museum—though I could
easily have been voted most likely to get kicked out of one. The
facts: I never studied art or art history, have zero experience of
any kind working in the art world, and have historically viewed
museums, and their staff, as kinda uptight, rule-bound you-
know-whats. Not to mention the fact that contemporary art in
particular always tripped me up. *Wait, I'm supposed to touch the
art? I'm NOT supposed to touch the art? And how am I supposed
to even figure out whether what I'm looking at IS the art? If there is
one crumpled candy wrapper on the museum floor it's garbage, but*

if a whole pile of candy is sitting in the corner of a gallery, it's art?
(Note: Candy piled in a corner is actually a well-known piece of
art by Felix Gonzalez-Torres. And, yes, you can touch and even
eat the candy.)

I suppose my ignorance at the time was understandable given
that the only real exposure I had to contemporary art growing up
was the folk art festivals my mom used to take me and my sibs to;
and I'm here to tell you that a clay cookie jar with a scrunched-
up cowboy face stuck on it and a big ol' cork shaped like a Stet-
son pushed through the top of said cowboy's head is not, despite
being made in the eighties, what museums mean by "contemporary art."

In any case, it turned out that my complete and utter be-
fuddlement about the art world was actually *why* I had been offered the job in the first place. One day, totally out of the blue,
I received a call from the director of the museum at the time,
Tim Rodgers, asking if I might be interested in being in charge
of turning a traditional gallery space within the museum into
a new kind of forum for artistic expression that would disrupt
all the usual conventions of museum-going. Tim was looking
for a rule-breaking outsider to activate a stunning new museum
space with new programs, audiences, and revenue streams, and I
was looking for a new challenge. So despite a healthy amount of
trepidation, I decided to give it a shot.

That's how I found myself sitting in Tim's sleek corner office dressed like a cartoon character and awaiting instructions
for my first day as the resident rule breaker. Tim, a bald man
in his fifties with a strong chin and impeccable posture, sat
perched behind an angular glass desk reading (what else?) an
Artforum magazine.

"Welcome," Tim said, surveying his stark white kingdom.
"We're excited to have you here."

"I'm excited to be here!" I said with a big smile intended to distract him from my noticeable jitters.

"Fantastic," Tim said, getting up from behind his desk. "Let me introduce you to the team and show you to your office."

Before I could muster the courage to tell him this had all been a big mistake, that I couldn't even properly curate my wardrobe, let alone a big beautiful gallery space (unless they had their sights set on a cowboy folk-art cookie-jar installation), he was marching me off to meet my new colleagues. The thinly veiled shock on the faces of my prim and proper new coworkers as Tim introduced me like a proud father who had just sprung his daughter from juvie said it all.

"This is Tania Katan, we hired her because she's a (*barely suppressing his mischievous grin*) . . . disruptor!"

"This is Tania, we brought her in because this museum needs some new energy and she writes and performs (*now really getting titillated*) . . . edgy stories!"

"This is Tania Katan and she is going to create (*on the verge of a full-on emission*) INNOVATIVE programs!"

And then the grand finale: "This is Tania and she thinks OUTSIDE the box!"

With the awkward meet-and-greets behind us, Tim showed me to my "office," which was in fact a cubicle. A very *small* cubicle, maybe two feet by three-and-a-half feet, tops. When I stood in the middle with my arms extended, like a scarecrow, I could almost touch the two opposite walls at once. I was fairly certain this was the smallest office that employees can legally be placed in. Just as I was pondering the size of my new work space relative to the average prison cell, I heard bloodcurdling screams! "What's that?" I asked Tim.

"Oh. Ice cream cake. The staff is celebrating a birthday. They usually get regular cake, so they're just really excited," he explained. "Welcome to the museum," he said cheerfully, as he turned back in the direction of his palatial office.

I stepped out of my cell. Paced the corridor. Wished I was a smoker. I stepped back inside and realized the chances were pretty high that I was going to lose my mind in this job. Taking a deep breath, I told myself that I had no choice but to get "lost" on my way back from lunch. Still, that was three whole hours away. In that moment of occupational despair, I did the only thing I knew how to do, the thing that any good practitioner of classical theater would do when the slings and arrows of outrageous fortune were hitting her directly in the pie hole . . . I launched into a soliloquy. A soliloquy, as you may know from *Hamlet*, is when one talks to oneself, aloud, because one is losing one's shit.

Okay, Tania, it looks like you have a BIG problem! How the hell are you supposed to create innovative programs in a big, beautiful empty space when you are trapped inside a teeny, tiny, squalid space? And isn't it ironic that you were hired to "think outside the box" and now he expects you to think from inside a tiny little box? Which resides inside a larger box: the museum itself. Whoa. This is so meta. Question: Did you already sign the contract? Answer: You are me, so you know we did! Another question: Doesn't Tim look like The Master from Doctor Who, *only with less hair? OMG, he hired you to control your mind, that's why he stuck you in a box!*

At some point during my one-woman performance, I had the most startling epiphany. *Maybe the key to thinking outside the box WAS to think inside the box.* I looked around for clues. Cubicles, I noted, have no ceilings. And when there are no ceilings . . . there are no limits!

In that moment, I had two powerful insights that inspired me to stay through lunch (and a few years after that too).

1. *Contrary to what my new boss seemed to believe, my theater training had actually prepared me for thinking INSIDE the box, not outside it. Theater LOVES boxes. We have box offices, black box theaters . . . hell, we even have box seats. I know my way inside and outside of a box! That sounded dirty. But get your mind out of the gutter. You know what I mean.*

2. *The less imaginative our physical office—or our job or title or role—the more essential our imagination becomes.*

This is our work as Creative Trespassers: sneaking imagination into tiny confined places with four walls—and breaking those walls down, making room for our creative ideas that have no bounds.

In the spirit of these realizations, the first program I created in my role as resident "disruptor" was an online series called "Out of the Cubicle." I hired a videographer, and once a week, the two of us would break out of my cubicle and sneak around the other offices making short, punchy videos that poked fun at, while also celebrated, the very art institution I worked for. My goal was to engage colleagues in playful interactions during the workday, while at the same time show viewers who thought (like I once had) that museums were stodgy and unapproachable can also be inviting, playful, and inclusive places, accessible to everyone. Sure, there were some colleagues who saw me running around the compound with joy and purpose and immediately reported me to my boss as well as to the board of directors, on the grounds that "She's not working, she's just having fun." As if the two were mutually exclusive. In any case, I respectfully noted their disapproval and carried on.

In the first episode, I decided to run for Employee of the

Month, launching a full-on Tracy Flick–style campaign (only very slightly less psycho). In another episode, I invited the distinguished architect Will Bruder (who had designed the entire museum) to redesign my crappy two-by-three-and-a-half-foot cubicle and filmed the "extreme office makeover" process.

THE LESS IMAGINATIVE OUR JOB, THE MORE ESSENTIAL OUR IMAGINATION BECOMES.

We launched the videos with zero marketing dollars—no splashy ads, no blast to a giant email list (we didn't even have a small email list), and no PR team. We did it the old-fashioned way: we posted the videos on Facebook. Then we picked up our phones, texted friends and colleagues a link to watch the videos, and hoped a handful would. Then something unexpected happened: Our friends didn't just *watch* the videos, they shared them. And then the people they shared them with shared them, and then *those* people shared them, and pretty soon visitors from all over the world—California, Missouri, New York, Iceland, Mexico, England, Italy—were streaming into the museum because they had seen these wacky videos and wanted to find out for themselves what this Scottsdale Museum of Contemporary Art place was all about.

The appeal of the videos was simple: They showed people that the art world, and those who work in it, are just as silly, awkward, ordinary, *and* extraordinary as anyone in any other profession can be. My original goal had been to break down the walls of my little cubicle to let creativity in, but in the end we actually ended up breaking down the walls of the entire museum and inviting the world in!

The lesson for you as a Creative Trespasser is this: No matter how unsexy your industry, how uninspiring your job title, or how small your cubicle, you too can find ways to break down the walls and let your imagination in.

The next challenge, once we had piqued people's interest in the museum, was the beautiful real-life space. One minor issue: I had never actually created and/or produced programs for, um . . . any space before. Although I had written plays and performed onstage, I'd never coordinated the lighting, box office, marketing, sales, costumes, or anything else. My responsibilities had been limited to writing, rewriting, memorizing my lines, and getting to the theater on time. But this was a whole new ball game.

So, I turned to theater history for a little guidance, more specifically the black box theater. Black box theaters were the disruptors of the theater world when they came on the scene in the 1960s, because instead of framing the action of a play onstage, in a theater, with all the uniform chairs in a row and facing forward, black box theaters busted out of that conventional frame, transforming small—sometimes crappy—spaces like storefronts with low ceilings, poor lighting, and just a mishmash of office-grade folding chairs scattered about for seating into immersive theatrical experiences. If we could find a way to emulate a black box theater instead of a traditional stage, I figured, all we needed was an idea, an audience, and some moxie!

I had moxie in spades, but what I *didn't* have was a clue about what kind of performance could draw an audience. After all, if you post a video online and no one watches it, it's like a tree falling in the forest, but when you invite people into an empty physical space and they don't show up . . . well, it's kinda noticeable. So I thought it would be useful to panic and then launch into another soliloquy.

Okay, let's start with the foundation for your job: Breaking the rules of a museum. We can work with that. How about a program for day drinking in the museum? That would be fun! But let's aim higher. Let's break one rule of the art world: how we acquire art. If you have money, you can acquire art, and if you don't, you can't. That's not fair. Lots of people love art and don't have the money to buy it. What if there was another way to acquire art? How did we acquire stuff before we had money, when we were kids? When we were kids our currency was speed, intelligence, and brawn; we would outrun, outwit, or outmuscle our opponent to win the prize. I got it . . . arm wrestling.

With a teeny part of my tiny annual budget, I bought me a "semi-professional arm wrestling table" online and plunked it right in the middle of the stark gallery space. Then I came up with a snappy name and tagline for the event: "Arm Wrestling for Art . . . Sometimes you've got to get abject to win an object." Then, because I didn't have a team, I took permission to assemble one: a videographer, an AV person, an intern, the museum security guards, the front-desk staff, a few docents, and a professional arm wrestler and fitness expert to teach proper technique to attendees. In the name of R&D, I also entered an arm-wrestling competition at a shopping mall, and I don't mean to brag, but . . . let's just say I enjoyed celebrating my victory over a couple of Cinnabons. True, my opponent was a wiry teenager, but still, she was really strong.

Finally, I asked a well-known artist to make a piece of art that we would give away, procured a curator to speak at the event, set the date, and prayed that people (other than members of my immediate family) would actually show up to a museum to strong-arm each other for a chance of winning an original piece of contemporary art. Luckily, the artist who generously agreed to make a piece for this event was none other than Eric Fischl, one of the most highly regarded American painters alive and kicking ass today. But still. *Arm wrestling in a museum??* And worse, a museum giving away art! What would the board of directors say? I'd been hired to break the rules, but was it possible I'd gone too far?

Friday night at 7:00 p.m., SMoCA opened its doors for the first-ever Arm Wrestling for Art. I was pacing. In fact, I had been pacing the slick concrete museum floors since 4:00 p.m., while simultaneously praying to the god of small things that people would show up. Please.

At 7:03 p.m., I was close to hyperventilating, due to the fact that if no one showed up, I would be humiliated and probably fired. At 7:08 p.m., four people excitedly burst through the doors. At 7:10 p.m., a few more arrived. By 7:15, waves of people were rolling in: people from the fitness community, museum donors, couples on first dates, grandmothers, artists, local business owners, board members, and more filled our empty space to capacity. They came, they trash-talked, they threw down, they had fun, and best of all, they came back—and brought their friends—to future museum events.

When you go out on a limb, there will always be doubters and naysayers who try to get you to stick to the way things "should" be done. But as a Creative Trespasser, you can bust out of the frames of mind that keep you stuck. You can reject the notion that you can only engage an audience and get them to suspend disbelief in a certain venue, in a certain way. No matter what you do or where you work, you can stage your own in-the-box performances in out-of-the-box ways. Here are a few ideas to try.

BUST THROUGH WALLS, CEILINGS, AND LIMITS

If there's one thing I've learned over a decade of helping people sneak creativity into their work, it's that we get to choose how we meet the expectations and goals of the organization. Sure, we know that the report will always be due, the budget will always be smaller than the scope of work, results will always need to be quantified and qualified, and our teams will always face challenges. But we also know that there are endless ways to get the report finished, to stretch the budget, to get the desired results, and to overcome the challenges. Creative Trespassers take the initiative to form our own teams, disrupt typical thinking, find new ways to acquire metrics, do more with less, and show the world what's possible.

My friend and mentor Dan Tyre, who was part of HubSpot's founding team and has successfully grown several companies from zero to bazillions of bucks, believes in "giving people playbooks, not scripts." He lets his teams know what the desired outcome is, and instead of telling them how to get there, he gives them the space and support to take initiative and pave their own creative ways.

So, if you're feeling trapped—whether it's inside a small cubicle, a huge organization, or a self-limiting direction or mindset—remember that "to be, or not to be" stuck is a choice that we make every single day. We may not get to choose whether we work in a tiny cubicle or a corner office, but we do get to choose whether to be confined by those physical walls, those organizational hierarchies, those narrow ways of thinking—or not. So, look up and remember . . . No ceiling, no limits!

KEEP MAKING STRANGE

I remember taking a cultural anthropology class in college where the professor had us describe our typical daily rituals to someone who had just landed on this planet. So, for example: We use a sharp tool to hack off the tough shells that cover our fingers (clipping nails). We hurl our bodies toward other bodies, at eighty miles per hour, from inside a pod made out of steel and aluminum (driving). This exercise radically shifted the way I saw mundane customs and turned them into weird, wonderful, and often awe-inspiring activities.

Another way to practice breaking out of your mental frameworks is to be a cultural anthropologist of your workplace. Go out into "the field" with a notebook, a pencil, and fresh eyes. Approach typical work rituals like an objective, empathic outsider; how would you describe them to someone who knew nothing about your work culture?

Or, as my friend Casandra Hernandez, an anthropologist by training and executive director of the arts organization Celebración Artística de las Américas, says, "The job of anthropologists is to make the strange familiar and the familiar strange. As artists, it's our job to keep making strange."

REHAB YOUR WORK SPACE

When you find that the doom and gloom of your office or cubicle is just too much to handle, instead of waiting for your work space to inspire you, create an inspired work space. There's a marketing director I know who places a candy jar with a chalkboard panel on it on the corner of her desk. Each week there is a fresh jar of candy and a new quote written on the chalkboard to inspire a conversation. If you walk past her desk, you get an inspirational quote and a mini–chocolate bar in exchange for a conversation.

SEEK THE STRANGE IN THE FAMILIAR. THE MOST EXTRAORDINARY IDEAS CAN OFTEN BE FOUND IN THE MOST ORDINARY SPACES.

You could decorate the outside of your cubicle or the door of your office with wrapping paper to remind yourself and others that the gift of creativity can be found inside. Or you could make Cubicle Sale signs and place them outside the office building with arrows leading to your cubicle, where you hold a garage sale, inviting coworkers to clear their heads by clearing out their clutter and donating all the random stuff that's been piling up in their work space or office. Then take everyone out to a nice lunch with the profits or donate them to a cause.

You can wallpaper the naked walls of your cubicle to give it a more homey feeling, or take sheets of paper, fill them with all the ideas that your cubicle can no longer contain, and stick them on the outside of your work space. Once, a colleague of mine surprised me for my birthday with a set of saloon doors—made out of old cardboard boxes—for my cubicle. Really, you can do anything as long as it sparks connection and conversation, isn't a fire hazard, and helps people see the familiar in a new light.

I used to occasionally place brass stanchions with red velvet ropes like theaters and nightclubs use for crowd control (which I bought at a garage sale) in front of my cubicle, to suggest something exciting is going to happen at any moment. I've even harnessed the power of sticky notes to wake up the joint. At the time, my office was less an office, per se, than an obscenely small cubicle with a window that happened to face out into the main corridor, which meant that all employees had to walk past my window in order to get to their respective offices. Here was the same group of people, who all worked for the same organization, people I saw every day, who I spent more time around than most of my family members, and yet as they shuffled past my window anonymously, I realized we knew nothing about each other. That's when I decided to strike up a visual conversation. So I started leaving sticky notes on the window, facing outward, that said things like: Ever feel like people just pass you by? What would you tell them if they stopped to listen?

Pretty soon, people from all departments and all levels of the company—including the CEO, head of HR, and other bigwigs—were leaving sticky-notes; not just answers, but also more questions, poetry, and drawings! Even those who weren't yet ready to leave their mark stopped to read the sticky-note constellation.

These little notes were fostering some pretty amazing connections among coworkers, who were often found chatting about the next image, poem, or question they were going to stick on the window. Coworkers sent me emails telling me how they used to feel a twinge of dread when passing through the corridor en route to their desks in the morning but now looked forward to seeing what was new on the window. These little notes changed the way we entered our work space. They reframed our workday as an opportunity to have a conversation, to collaborate, to look for extraordinary ideas in ordinary spaces.

Productive Disruption

1. Grab a sticky note.
2. Write a message to inspire, support, or connect with a human (or humans) you work with.
3. Stick it!
4. Invite others to do the same.

SNEAK ART INTO UNLIKELY SPACES

Whether you think of yourself as artistic or not, surrounding yourself with art—whether it's paintings, photography, or something a little more avant-garde—can be a powerful force for transformation. And no matter where you work or what you do, you can find a way to infuse art into your physical space.

For artist Rick Lowe, sneaking art into places you'd least expect it was an inside job. In 1993, Lowe, along with six other African American artist-collaborators, all living in Houston, took a hard look at Houston's historic Third Ward community, a predominantly African American neighborhood filled with poverty, high crime rates, and dilapidated houses. Once there, they decided it was time to answer their own collective question: How can art be an engine for social transformation? The answer came in the form of Project Row House, a project that has transformed the houses that were once falling apart into vibrant community centers filled with art, artist residencies, and other programs, all with the goal, as their website put it, of serving "young single mothers with the ambition of a better life for themselves and their children, small enterprises with the drive to take their businesses to the next level, and artists interested in using their talents to understand and enrich the lives of others."

Sneaking art into unlikely spaces—whether those spaces are former low-income housing projects or the walls of your office or cubicle—can be transformational. It can help you gain new perspectives, envision a broader range of future outcomes, open your mind, and inspire you to use your own creativity in novel and unexpected ways—ones that just might enrich the lives of others in the process.

CHAPTER 8

LOSE THE MAP,
FIND YOUR SENSE OF DIRECTION

Sometimes I think creativity is magic;
it's not a matter of finding an idea, but
allowing the idea to find you!

—MAYA LIN, *Artist and Architect*

MY ENTIRE FAMILY was blessed with a great sense of direction. Everyone, that is, except for me. When I was a kid, my family nicknamed me Navigationally Challenged. Let's just say that finding my way with a map was not an area where I tended to shine. Truth be told, I couldn't even *locate* most places on a map. But don't cry for me, Argentina (wherever that is!); I shone in other areas, like writing silly skits, doing impressions of *SNL* characters, and cracking jokes on long car rides.

So whenever we would drive to a new town or city or even an unfamiliar shopping mall, I would busy myself telling jokes to an audience of no one in the backseat while my mom confidently whipped out a map. She, my brother, and my sister would then become a team of cartographers, studiously examining the intricate lines and color-coded keys and deftly figuring out the lay of the land. No matter where we found ourselves, they somehow managed to point out the important landmarks (i.e., lunch spots), find the public restrooms, lead us back to the car, and get us safely home before I could utter "Where are we?"

Although I loved exploring new places, locating them ahead of time by staring at a dizzying array of indistinguishable lines made my brain glaze over. At the ripe old age of twelve, it was clear to me that you were either born with the navigation gene or condemned to be poked fun at for not having it, so I gave up on trying to find my way and went back to perfecting my Roseanne Roseannadanna impression instead.

When I grew up and moved to Los Angeles, my poor sense of direction graduated from mild inconvenience to debilitating affliction. Without my map-savvy mother and siblings to help me get around, I had to figure out a system that empowered me to leave my home and find my way to work, *by myself*, without freaking out the whole way there. Mind you, this was before cell phones, MapQuest, and Google Maps. This was in the olden days when if you wanted a "street view" you had to get up off your ass and walk out into the street. Back then, the closest thing to a navigation "app" was the *Thomas Guide*, a twenty-pound, spiral-bound book containing maps of every city in the United States drawn in a manner so intricate and overwhelming that they looked like they came straight out of the baroque period.

My system consisted of spending hours translating the *Thomas Guide* into something that made sense in my directionally challenged head. I'd take a scrap of paper and draw a long curved line from here to there, adding a few crude drawings of parks and landmarks I'd encounter along the way. Chicken-scratched street names and freeway numbers followed. Then, for good measure, I'd create a mnemonic device based on song lyrics to guide me on my journey. Right Turn on Ventura Boulevard was prompted by Tom Petty ("All the vampires, walkin' through the valley, move west down Ventura Boulevard"). Exit on Hollywood Boulevard was led by Bob Seger ("And those Hollywood nights, in those Hollywood hills"). A meeting on Sunset was "You caught yourself a trick down on Sunset and Vine" by David Bowie. These too got transcribed onto my scrap of paper in barely legible handwriting.

By the time I was finished creating my "map," it looked like it was made by someone who spent a decade in solitary confinement for a crime they didn't commit, or perhaps a three-year-old who accidentally found and ate her parents' entire stash of hash cookies.

In any case, pretty much anytime I had to leave the house, I'd get into my car and carefully place that janky scrap of paper on my lap so I could consult it while driving on the ol' 405. True, driving on L.A. freeways can be treacherous enough when keeping one's eyes on the road, let alone looking down at one's crotch for directions, but hey, it was all I could come up with. At this point, perhaps you're wondering "Did that little scrap of paper ever fly out the window of your green Geo Metro, which naturally you kept open because you didn't have air conditioning?"

Yes. Yes, it did. In fact, said scrap tried to escape several times, which compelled me to pull off the freeway, jump out of my car, and ask random pedestrians and burned-out store clerks questions such as "How do I get to Hollywood?"

Somehow, despite these setbacks, my homespun hieroglyphics got me all the way through my twenties. So by the time I hit my thirties and got an invitation to travel to Venice, Italy, I was confident that my unconventional navigational tactics and I were ready to *carta geografica* our way to the floating city!

If you've ever had the privilege of going to Venice, or reading Italo Calvino's *Invisible Cities*, you know that there is no map up to the challenge of guiding you through the labyrinthine maze of canals and alleyways. I'd venture to say that even the sturdy *Thomas Guide* is no match for the tangled twists and turns of Venice, nor the unexpected dead ends that drop you off at the edge of the Adriatic Sea.

Anyhow, since I hadn't read *Invisible Cities* or been to Venice, when I stepped foot on those beautifully crooked cobblestones for the first time and looked out onto the sea, I thought, "This is my city!" Then I promptly got lost. Not even on my way to a museum or to gelato or anything awesome, just walking to the hotel. Okay, I thought, I'll just ask pedestrians for directions. Except that I didn't speak Italian fluently, or even weakly. All I knew were the few choice phrases I had learned from a snarky friend who had lived in Italy: "Give me a cappuccino." "Pig misery" (aka "Shit!"). And "Check, please." Which, if strung together, made a certain kind of sense but didn't really help me find my way.

As I wandered the windy streets, getting lost at every turn, my feet were aching and the weight of my backpack was literally bringing me down, so I found a neighborhood bar, sat down, and drank a cold prosecco. Thanks to the bubbles and my new-found sense of alcohol-induced calm, I was soon ready to press on. Within a few blocks, I was of course lost again. But instead of giving up, I just kept walking, trusting my internal compass, following the twists and turns rather than resisting their pull. And once I did, these same streets that had, just an hour before, made me want to scream *"Porca miseria!"* led me to the most beautiful neighborhoods, churches, and synagogues I'd ever set eyes on, the best gelato and pizza I've ever eaten. Even museums I longed to visit somehow appeared in front of me. Getting lost was pure magic. My inability to find my way out of a paper bag wasn't a personal failing, I realized; it was an art form.

When the sun started to fall, I asked a shop owner—thankfully one who spoke English—for directions to my hotel, telling him that I spent the whole day happily lost. He smiled knowingly and said, "If you get lost, you look up." Of course! This dude was the sage of Venice! When surrounded by the most exquisite architecture, ancient ruins dating back to the first century, majestic bell towers, and piazzas with the patina of visionary painters, designers, and literati who have shaped arts and letters the world over, I mused aloud, the last thing you want to be doing is looking down at a map! "*Grazie!*" I proclaimed, and began to leave. "No, no," he called out behind me, "I meant, you look up at the signs on buildings."

Sure enough, there were signs—with clear arrows—for every major landmark stuck on the sides of buildings. San Marco, Ferrovia, Piazzale Roma.

Okay, so maybe he wasn't a sage per se, but he did point me in the right direction, both literally and figuratively. He showed me the value in looking up and in letting the signs guide my path. It turns out, Venice is my city after all. It's a city that demands you throw out the map and trust your internal guide. It's a city that forces you to learn one of the most important life lessons there is: Getting lost is how we end up finding our own unique way.

Creative Trespassers live by these words as though they were tattooed on our forearms. We don't need no stinking maps, because we have something better than a map, we've got an IGS, an inner guidance system. It's kind of like a GPS, but instead of satellite signals, it uses our most deeply held convictions, instincts, and values to guide us and help us find our way. Bonus, it doesn't talk to us in a creepy human-computer voice, and instead of steering us to the closest freeway entrance, it helps us locate the stuff we live for, stand up for at all costs, our reasons for being. Our *why* and our *how* all wrapped into one. As the bestselling author Simon Sinek skillfully explained in his book *Start with Why*, *why* is our reason. So if *why* is our reason, then *how* is our way. Our inner guidance system is what steers us as we travel from *why* to *how*. It is our bridge from our purpose to our plan.

GETTING LOST IS HOW WE END UP FINDING OUR OWN UNIQUE WAY.

It's time to admit that your inner guidance system has been on this whole time, whether you've been listening to it or not. Yep, it's been talking to you in an encouraging voice for years, signaling, "It's clear, you can follow your passions now!" And you're like, "I should know exactly where I'm going first." And your IGS is like, "Try any direction, all roads lead to you finding out something new about yourself." And you're like, "Well, I really should know where I'm going before I go. What if I choose the wrong passion to follow? Or, worse, what if I can't find my purpose?!" And your IGS is like, "There's no such thing as the wrong passion. And you don't have just ONE purpose, you've got a bunch—now GO. Trust the process!" And you're like, "Just give me a clue, dammit!" And that's when your IGS is like,

"Forget it, I'm gonna go guide someone who's ready to rock the cosmos! Peace out."

The best thing about your inner guidance system: It's always turned on and ready to help you rock. You never need to charge that sucker or get batteries for it or pay a monthly service fee; it's up and running as long as you are. All you need to do is embody your values and let that baby do the rest. Whether you're part of the C suite or a corporate foot soldier, embodying your values at work will allow you to explore and get lost without losing your way. It will profoundly shift the way in which you contribute, lead, and listen, and put the life back into your work life!

EMPATHY LOVES COMPANY

A friend of mine, who is the director of corporate communications for a Fortune 100 retailer (and card-carrying Creative Trespasser), once stole something from the company he used to work for. He admitted to the thievery after we had a conversation about what values we bring with us from job to job. Turned out that what he had stolen from his previous employer wasn't a stapler or a ream of printer paper; he stole a value instead. The value in question: empathy. Damn, what a great value to nab! All the more so because at the time, his new team was struggling to find creative ways to engage customers. He knew that if his team learned how to put themselves in those customers' shoes, they could come up with more innovative ways to deliver value.

So, he held offsite meetings where everyone shared a meal as well as their own best and worst experiences as customers, everything from those moments when they wanted to throw in the microfiber bath towel instead of buying it, to those times when they felt swaddled in the luxury of Egyptian cotton as they were seen, respected, and guided through the buying process.

Although empathy didn't make its way into the company's official core values statement, it did quickly become a core value for the customer service team. This new approach improved sales, increased the number of satisfied customers, and motivated more team members to be more proactive and creative in their approach to customer service. When it came time for performance reviews, those team members who showed a deep understanding and implementation of empathy knocked it out of the park!

The best leaders, the most prolific artists and writers, the most inspiring change agents steal values all the time. Another great example is from an artist named Ann Morton, who nabbed a value that she'd observed in her parents while growing up— dignity—and took it to the streets. Driven by a desire to recognize the valuable people and objects that have been forgotten and discarded in our communities, Morton created an ongoing project called Street Gems, which invites individuals with a history of chronic homelessness to make art out of plastic bottles, cups, and lids found littering the streets. Sometimes convening in outdoor spaces and other times in community centers, Morton and her community of collaborators bend, shape, and reconstruct the cast-off plastic into beautiful necklaces, earrings, and whimsical "flowers," and sell them to the public. In exchange for turning garbage into art, her collaborators are paid, remembered, and treated with dignity.

The eighth commandment aside, stealing (though personally I prefer the term *borrowing*) a value or values that you admire in someone—be it a former employer, a friend, a family member, an ex, an artist, a writer, or a social movement—can help you build that bridge from *why* to *how*; it can lead you to head in new directions without straying from what you stand for.

Productive Disruption

1. Nab a value from someone you admire.

2. Bring it to work.

3. Live it.

4. Share it.

STAND UP FOR CORE VALUES (LITERALLY)

I met Stacy Kirk (CEO of QualityWorks Consulting Group) when we were on a panel together. I knew I had to get to know this woman better, ASAP, when she answered a question about the value she brought to her company by replying, "My value in the world is greater than my fears." I'm pretty sure I then turned to her and mouthed, "Who are YOU?!"

Having a gut feeling that I was in the presence of a fellow Creative Trespasser, I asked her if she had any sneaky strategies for keeping herself and her team committed to standing up for their (and the company's) values. Hell, yeah, she did! Literally.

As employees of a company that creates tools and frameworks to accelerate software delivery, her team quite naturally values an agile way of working. This means they value thinking, moving, and collaborating quickly, efficiently, nimbly: always being on their toes. That's why they do stand-up meetings. If you're not familiar with a stand-up meeting, it's one where the whole team literally stands, and each member has one minute or so to share only necessary information about where they are on a project, what they've finished, and what they plan on tackling next. The whole standing thing ensures that people communicate efficiently; when these meetings are jamming, you can get in and out in fifteen minutes or less.

You might assume that standing meetings proved a challenge for Stacy, given that half her team was located in the U.S. and the other half in Jamaica. But Stacy had a creative solution to this problem at the ready: video conferencing. One day, however, after Stacy's team in Jamaica noticed that the past few meetings had been dragging, they decided to kick things up a notch. So this time, when the U.S.-based team answered the video call, they were treated to a little surprise: Instead of standing, their Jamaican colleagues were stretched out, faces to the floor, in plank position. Talk about agile!

Now, whenever their stand-ups are dragging on and they want people to sweat out that necessary information fast, they drop into plank position. Strengthening their commitment to their core principles (while also strengthening their core) helps keep them focused on being the most agile, nimble, and productive team possible.

LEAVE A CREATIVE LEGACY

Not all jobs are built to last. Sometimes we find ourselves blindsided, whether by unrealistic expectations, people being "let go" during lunch, or a lack of raises year after year and eventually the lightbulb goes off and we realize it's definitely time to leave. The question is: What will you leave behind? Will you leave a big old F-you as payback for your frustration and fury in the form of dirty dishes, empty ink cartridges, and a pert middle finger for your boss? Or will you choose to leave a creative legacy that might inspire and enliven future employees? In theater, how we exit a scene is just as important as how we enter. Both in theater and in careers, our exits show the audience whether we've grown, stayed stuck, or been transformed along the way.

Now, choosing to leave things better than when you arrived at a job is some next-level take-the-high-road shit, so if you're not ready, that's cool. But why not try to leave something behind that will improve conditions and processes for your fellow humans? Instead of making off with a year's supply of notepads, for example, how about leaving a note for your replacement outlining where things stand on various ongoing projects and inviting her to write you at your personal email if she has questions?

Leaving a big F-you, or leaving a creative legacy. One will get you a one-finger salute, while the other might help you land a new opportunity. The choice is yours.

HUMANIZE CONNECTIVITY

Expedia Worldwide Engineering, a division of Expedia Inc., once brought me into its annual Feedback Forum to share disruptive strategies for infusing more creativity into the role of leadership. About four hundred engineers, all senior level, from around the globe converged in Bellevue, Washington, to explore what they were doing well and how they could do better, specifically when it came to leading with one of their core values: *seeking new ideas, different ways of thinking, diverse backgrounds and approaches.*

When my presentation was finished, we opened the floor up for Q&A, and I was totally caught off guard when several people expressed that their biggest concern was their difficulty connecting in real life with their counterparts around the world. Given that these were pragmatic engineers at a fast-moving, iterative tech company, however, "real life" actually meant video conferencing, which is why their question for me was: "How do we disrupt video conferencing to really connect?"

Intuitively, they knew the value of connecting with colleagues from diverse backgrounds—people who challenge us and change the way we think—to share ideas and innovate in real time and space. But they didn't know how. In that moment, the solution became obvious to me: pen pals. I suggested that they start becoming pen pals with their overseas colleagues. I mean, Expedia used technology to disrupt the way we travel overseas, so it only seemed fitting for them to use good old-fashioned analog mail to disrupt the way they connected with other human beings overseas. Plus, what better way to get a true sense of someone than through the way they write, the stamps they choose, by picturing them sitting at a desk thousands of miles away, putting words on the same piece of paper you now hold in your hands? Not to mention the bonus thrill of running to the mailbox in anticipation of receiving a letter! The engineers loved it, and more importantly, the exercise helped them forge stronger connections and generate more creative ideas that continue to bridge the oceans, continents, and cultural differences between them.

Productive Disruption

1. Find a pen pal. It could be a colleague at a different branch in your company, a relative, a friend, someone in your field that you admire, or anyone else as long as they live in a city, country, or continent you've never visited.
2. Write (by hand) and physically send letters to your pen pal (no email, social media, or other tech interfaces).
3. Bonus: Make it a goal to go visit their city, country, continent within the next five years.

CHAPTER 9
UNLEASH
YOUR INNER REBEL

The only way to deal with an unfree world is to become so absolutely free that your very existence is an act of rebellion.

—ALBERT CAMUS, *Philosopher and Author*

SOMETIMES THE GREATEST act of resistance is to stand up and fully lean into our dreams. Standing up requires us to cultivate a state of mind, one where we believe that our voice matters. That our ideas matter. That we matter.

As Creative Trespassers, we stand up every time we trust our creative impulses. We stand up when we declare our intentions with clarity and courage. We stand up when we take action in honor of people, ideas, and causes. We stand up when we find connections between our company's mission statement and our personal one between our job and our work; between art and commerce. We stand up when we trade indifference and inertia for imagination and inspiration.

So think of this chapter as the ultimate throwdown: our fears versus our dreams, our passions versus procrastination, our professional desires versus the desire to check social media just one more time! This is our time to kick the crap out of the stuff that is stopping us from living free. But first, let me tell you a little story about how my passion and procrastination faced off in a café and almost fought to the death.

STANDING UP REQUIRES US TO CULTIVATE A STATE OF MIND, ONE WHERE WE BELIEVE THAT OUR VOICE MATTERS. THAT OUR IDEAS MATTER. THAT WE MATTER.

It all began when I received an email with three thrilling—and terrifying—letters in the subject line: TED. It was an invitation to give a TEDx talk—a dream opportunity for a budding professional speaker such as myself. Immediately I said YES and then proceeded to drag my feet (and my ass), until I finally dragged myself to my office, where I would buckle down and lean into preparing the biggest talk of my entire professional life.

The problem was, whenever I tried to sit down and write, my creativity left the building, and in its place was a neon sign that read: DO STUFF THAT WILL DERAIL YOUR DREAMS! What a great idea! I heeded these divine instructions and dove into any form of procrastination I could conjure. Obsessively checking emails (hey, they aren't going to check themselves!). Doing laundry (clean underwear, what a gift!). Washing dishes (who knew how much fun it was to scrub hardened avocado from a spoon?!). Scrolling through social media (meh, but better than working). Snacking (yum). Soon the "breaks" started overtaking the writing, and since I was already at zero percent productivity, I went out to get a cup of coffee and maybe a fresh-baked vegan scone.

As I waited for my hot cup of avoidance, I ran into a friend's husband, Ray. Ray is a journalist, lean with language, very straightforward. "What are you working on these days?" he asked casually.

"I was just invited to give a TEDx talk," I said. "I'm trying to write it."

"How's it going?" he asked.

"It's not. I need someone who isn't me to give me a deadline. You deal with deadlines for a living, can you give me one?"

"Sure. How old are you?"

"Thirty-nine."

"Well . . . you don't have much time left."

Wow. There is nothing like the realization that you're gonna kick it to help kick you into high gear. Ray putting the *dead* in *deadline* really put my procrastination into perspective. Giving a TEDx talk had always been one of my biggest professional dreams. So why was I actively distracting myself from achieving it? It was like my passion and procrastination had confronted each other in a head-to-head battle for my energy and attention.

I imagine the showdown going something like this.

PROCRASTINATION: I can totally kick your ass! I'm just gonna do it tomorrow.

PASSION: Ha! I'm here to kick my own ass because I'm worth it!

PROCRASTINATION: Okay, overachiever, you win. Today. But tomorrow . . . I'm gonna get you and your doggie too.

If your passion and procrastination confronted each other at a café, who would you be rooting for? After running into Ray, it was glaringly clear who I needed to be cheering on: It was passion all the way! I put the pedal to the metal and started writing my talk.

Whether your passion is starting your own business, learning a new skill, traveling the world, giving a TEDx talk, or anything else, it's time to break free of those procrastination shackles and fly toward freedom! *No, I'm just gonna grab a snack first. No, hold on, let me just do a load of laundry. No, wait, I have to create a ghost Facebook account to keep track of my exes.* NO. THIS is your chance to rebel against your old patterns and enjoy a make-out session with your passions. THIS is your escape route from procrastination and stagnation, your chance to take one giant leap toward your dreams. Today we're gonna defy those inner voices that stop us from leaning into our awesomeness, because our dreams can't wait until tomorrow. It's time to put our passions front and center. TODAY.

MAKE A "TO-DON'T" LIST

Are there any pesky patterns of procrastination that are keeping you from pursuing your passion? (Holy alliteration, Wonder Woman!) It's okay, you can tell me. I've done 'em all! What do you do to avoid working toward achieving your dreams? Come on. Are you fixated on organizing your sock drawer, again? Obsessively filing away your emails to make room for the influx of new ones? Compulsive texting? Extreme snacking? What about checking ALL of your social media feeds? Twice?

It's your job as a Creative Trespasser to fail at the things you can do tomorrow and kick ass at all the things you choose to do today.

By consciously changing your habits, you change the trajectory of your life. You can choose to prioritize the things that enliven you rather than things that drag you down. You can choose to live your life with intention. Because with intention comes freedom.

FAIL AT THE THINGS YOU CAN DO TOMORROW AND KICK ASS AT ALL THE THINGS YOU CHOOSE TO DO TODAY.

Productive Disruption

1. Grab a piece of paper. Yes, a physical piece of paper, you'll see why.
2. On top write: TO-DON'T LIST.
3. Make a list of ALL the crap you do to avoid your dreams. Be honest and detailed.
4. Take your list along with a lighter or match and head to the toilet, fireplace, or backyard fire pit and . . . burn, baby, burn!
5. If you are feeling extra-rebellious, you can even host a burning party. Invite your coworkers over to make TO-DON'T LISTs together. Opening a can of whoop-ass on those nasty habits that are no longer serving you and making room for your passions is the best team-building exercise ever!

WRITE YOUR FIGHT SONG

Now that nothing is standing between us and our dreams, it's time for us Creative Trespassers to rise up and start a work culture revolution. And no one ever started a revolution from an armchair, so let's stand up and fight for what we believe in.

But first, we have to know what the heck we believe in, what our goals are, and how we're gonna make them a reality. It's time to create harmony between the work we do and who we are. It's time to make a declaration of independence about how we'll infuse our authentic self into what we do for our nine-to-five. It's time to write our fight song!

Every Trespasser who has ever stood up and started a revolution—transforming the way we think, act, care, collaborate, work, and live—has a fight song. Sometimes they call it a mission statement. Sometimes they call it a manifesto. This shit is so powerful that corporations have co-opted it. Every brand from Apple to Lululemon to Simple Shoes has a manifesto: a declaration and a road map all wrapped up into one.

The best part? You don't need a certification, an MBA, or a permission slip from your boss to write one. You just freaking grab it by the huevos and write it. How cool is that? Answer: VERY.

Maybe you're reading this and thinking, "A fight song? A manifesto? Those sound pretty intense. I just want to do my job with a little more joy and imagination." Well, allow me to offer some alternative language: It's like a road map for your life force, an action plan for your ambition, an onboarding process for your dreams. The bottom line is that by declaring your goals and articulating what you stand for, you'll be able to take meaningful steps today toward the future you imagine.

Like manifestos, mission statements, and other forms of creative expression, your fight song will have a few key components: vision, intentions, and action. By putting these words to paper, you give them power.

1. **Vision:** *Write down all the things you stand for, the people and causes you champion, the stuff you believe in at all costs.*

2. **Intentions:** *Write down what you hope to accomplish by bringing these beliefs into your everyday work. How will your days, your weeks, your life change for the better as a result of standing up for what you believe in?*

3. **Action:** *How are you gonna sneak your secret sauce into the office? List the small to large steps you'll take to make your vision a reality.*

4. **And last but not least . . .** *your rallying cry. Like the chorus of your favorite song, a rallying cry is that mighty phrase that makes us wanna dance, dare, and declare,* This is my fight song! *When we're too tired, scared, or discouraged to stand, a rallying cry reminds us that we are never standing alone. Consider what is perhaps the most famous rallying cry in history:* "I have a dream that one day this nation will rise up, live out the true meaning of its creed . . . I have a dream . . ."

So try firing up whatever music gets you pumped, setting a timer for fifteen minutes, and writing a fight song. Write without editing or judging. You can always go back and add, revise, or tweak, but it's important to go forward before you go backward.

For an example of what a Creative Trespasser's fight song might look like, here's part of mine. I started with I *stand for . . .*

I stand for risk-taking misfits, those who are brave enough to write their fight songs on company letterhead. I stand for pursuing our passions instead of postponing them; for chasing our dreams instead of derailing them. (Vision)

We are *Creative Trespassers and our job is productive disruptions! (Rallying Cry)*

Because we spend more than 40 percent of our life at work, I'm going to implement 40 percent more opportunities to be playful and imaginative during the workday. (Intentions)

I will start a Slack channel called #CreativeTrespassing for employees to share stories of sneaking creativity into the work space. I will subvert the sartorial by wearing sneakers even when it's not Casual Friday. (Action)

We are *Creative Trespassers and our job is productive disruptions! (Rallying Cry)*

Now it's your turn to create a living, breathing declaration of creative independence. And when you're finished, take your fight song out for a spin. Test it out on your spouse, your children, a friend, a trusted colleague, the mailman, your pet rock—whoever will listen. But be forewarned, once you feel the power of declaring what you stand for and how you intend to turn that vision into a reality, well, my friend, there are some side effects to be aware of. You might experience a sudden urge to stand up, jump up and down, pump your fists in the air, and solemnly swear to rock your truth, the whole truth, and nothing but the truth, so help you Kool Moe Dee. You might start humming the theme song to *Rocky* at work. You might even find yourself in the middle of your open workstation, in the middle of a workday, belting out your fight song, indoor voice be damned! That's cool, just tell your stunned colleagues that you're rewriting your life, no big whoop.

If you want to, print that sucker out and stick it on your soft cubicle wall. Make it your screen saver. Drink your watered-down work coffee out of a mug with your rallying cry screen-printed on it.

Write it, read it, live it, love it, rock it! This is your fight song, take back your life song: *We are* Creative *Trespassers and our job is productive disruptions!*

CHAPTER 10

KICK IMPOSTER
SYNDROME IN THE ARSE

I wondered if I would spend the rest of my life
inventing complicated ways to depress myself.
—MIRANDA JULY, *Filmmaker, Artist, and Writer*

SO, I'M ABOUT to get onstage at one of the largest tech conferences in the world, CiscoLive!, where I'm supposed to share some brilliant wisdom that will inspire thousands of people to embrace their inner superhero. No biggie. (Insert emoji face screaming in fear!)

Just so you know, I love public speaking. I always show up prepared, rehearsed, and ready to rock. Of course, that doesn't mean that I don't channel my inner scaredy-cat when staring out into a sea of faces belonging to smart, capable, and curious people from around the globe. And even though I love me a live audience, sometimes my nerves have the nerve to start acting up, especially when I am reminded that it's me, a five-foot-three-inch nerd with a tendency toward seasonal eczema (the flakes occur right between my eyes), about to tell a room full of REAL and largely acne-free superheroes how to be a . . . superhero. HOLY fraud, Batman!

In this particular instance, I was supposed to speak right after the senior vice president of Cisco Systems (you know, that lil' old multibillion-dollar company), and right before Lieutenant Carey Lohrenz, first female lieutenant to fly an F-14 Tomcat in the U.S. Navy. Talk about intimidating! The only tomcat I ever had anything to do with was Mitch, a mangy twenty-pound tabby who had two chewed-off ears and an attitude to match. And I've never been SVP or LT or even owned a BMW!! Once, I thought I had IBS, but that was just an unfortunate side effect of drinking too much coffee.

Anyway, so I'm about to go onstage, palms a little sweaty, trying to ignore the flashbacks I was having of the unfortunate incident with the tabby cat. "Don't worry," I tell myself, "it's not like I'm going to put one foot onstage and, in unison, the audience will call out 'BULLSHIT!' Right? Right?"

I climb up onto the stage. The floor feels solid beneath my feet. So far so good. I stare out into the sea of superheroes and ask, "Are there any superheroes here today?" I take a breath and continue, "That's right, we are all born superheroes, then we spend the rest of our lives apologizing for it." And just like that, I'm off and running.

The minutes pass faster than a locomotive, and the next thing I know, my speech is over. I exit the stage in a post-talk fog, and standing right there is the first female F-14 Tomcat fighter pilot in the flesh, who smiles at me and says, "How am I going to follow that? You were amazing!"

But here's the thing: Until that moment, I was totally convinced that I had blanked in the middle of my talk, or farted and tried to pass it off as my sneakers rubbing the stage floor, or used the F word while we were live streaming. I was positive that the wave of applause was actually an explosion of boooos, and that if the opportunity had presented itself, the audience would almost certainly have thrown rotten tomatoes at me.

Isn't it amazing how sometimes the only difference between

feeling like an imposter or a superhero is finding out how other people see you from the outside? But what if we could channel that objective outsider for ourselves all the time? Like what if we could carry a fighter pilot around in our pockets to constantly remind us how awesome we are? And we actually believed it, cuz she's so effing ace?!

And, just so you know—if you often feel like a fraud or phony and worry that someone is going to call bullshit on you at any moment, you're not alone. It's been proven that the MORE accomplished we are, the more likely we are to feel like an imposter. That makes no sense, right? I wouldn't have believed it either, except for the fact that the more I coach and consult with some of the most hardworking, intelligent, and super-successful business leaders, performers, and movers and shakers in so many different fields, the more I hear it: *I feel like an imposter; can you help me with that?* My first thought is always: *What? That's preposterous!* And then I realize, we ALL feel like an imposter sometimes. Like we just lucked out, and that's the only reason why we're running the company, speaking on the main stage, leading the trainings, and being given the opportunities. Or, worse, we might decide that we don't have enough credentials, knowledge, or experience to run the company, speak publicly, lead trainings, or get opportunities, so we don't even try, or we give up too quickly, or we tell ourselves that pursuing the things that enliven us the most isn't that important anyway.

The truth is, we are *all* a hard act to follow! So, if it's okay with you, can we call BULLSHIT on feeling like shit about ourselves and put a lid on those damn internal monologues once and for all?

It often takes an outsider who believes in us to see what we are capable of—but we can develop that capability inside ourselves too. We just gotta do our homework, develop our skills, and show up ready to rock—and continue to scale buildings like the superheroes we are.

And, hey, if you're not ready to embrace your inner superhero, at least do it for your kids or your nieces and nephews so they can see what it looks like to be scared and do it anyway. Do it for your colleagues, otherwise you're cheating them out of all the ideas, skills, and connections you've developed in your career that can help everyone take the company to the next level. Don't be stingy with your gifts! Here are some creative ways to call bullshit on fear and insecurity and rock out with your superpowers.

I *ROCK* FILES!

Remember *The Rockford Files?* That TV show from the seventies about a detective—Jim Rockford—who was imprisoned for a crime he didn't commit, then once he got released could only afford to live in some ramshackle trailer while trying to launch his career as a private eye? Let's just say he had some career setbacks, like we all do, and yet he still managed to ROCK his cases.

That's how he became my inspiration for an act of Creative Trespassing that I call the "I ROCK Files." So, no excuses, it's time to become a private detective hot on your own trail. Create a physical file (you can have a digital one too) and gather all kinds of evidence proving the unique value you bring to work with you. Slide a glowing performance review in there. A printout of an email from a colleague or boss that praises you for a "job well done!" Press clippings from events you helped produce, reports showing goals achieved or surpassed, thank-you cards from customers, awards, certificates, and so on. From teeny to extra-special, all evidence that points to you rocking it counts!

Now whenever you need a reminder that you rock, or need to hear it from an outside source, open up your file, read about one or more of your accomplishments, and mentally give yourself a high five. Then get back to rocking.

STOP COCKBLOCKING YOUR CAREER

> *Cockblock* is a slang term for an action, intentional or not, that serves to prevent someone from having [an awesome life].
>
> —WIKIPEDIA

OKAY, I SUBBED out *sex* for *an awesome life*, but same difference, except for the fact that sex lasts a few minutes (okay, maybe longer for some of you, but no need to be cocky about it), and a life obviously lasts much longer. Regardless, why do so many of us do things, intentionally or not, to cockblock ourselves in life, especially when it comes to our career? Here is a cautionary tale of career cockblocking that also shows how, with a few shifts, we can all move out of our own way and make way for awesomeness!

A coaching client of mine needed some guidance on transitioning careers. She had worked in technology years earlier, then moved into finance and now wanted to get back into the tech industry. She was interviewing for a position at a company I knew very well and asked for my insights about the organization, its culture, and so on. First, I assured her that no one currently working in that department had as much direct technology experience as she had. Secondly, I told her that I happened to know the salaries of the last two people who had been hired in that position: $70,000. And finally, I gave her a full-blown, rah-rah, pompoms-in-the-air pep talk, which wasn't difficult at all because she was in fact totally and uniquely qualified for the job. A few days later, the company invited her to be a part of the team. When they brought up salary, she asked for $55,000. They offered her $50,000. She took the job.

Why? Because even though she was more qualified for the job than the last two people in that position, she doubted herself and her experience. In other words, she had textbook imposter syndrome and, as a result, cockblocked her career to the tune of $20,000 in just that first year's salary alone.

How many times have you undersold yourself to your new or current employer? How many times have you known the numbers and undershot anyway? When we do, not only are we leaving free cash on the table, but we're telling ourselves (and everyone around us) we don't value our abilities.

Next time, try admitting that you are worth it. Admit that you have put in the work. Admit that you are uniquely qualified for this career opportunity. Admit to your awesomeness. Admit it again. One more time. The more we admit that we have value, the more valuable opportunities present themselves. So stop cockblocking yourself, and get out there and seize those opportunities by the balls.

ASSEMBLE A LEGION OF SUPERHEROES

You know how corporations have a board of directors to (in theory) make the company stronger, maintain checks and balances, and leverage resources, to help advance the organization's vision? Well, why not assemble your own personal board of directors to leverage resources to advance your vision, keep you in check and balanced, and help make your career stronger? My friend Alison Wade, president of Conferences, Training, and Consulting for Techwell, calls her personal board of directors her "front row" because those are people she invites to sit spitting distance from the stage, cheer her on, challenge her, and review her performance. I call mine my Legion of Super-heroes, because I dig the idea of joining forces to do good in the corporate galaxy.

THE MORE WE ADMIT THAT WE HAVE VALUE, THE MORE VALUABLE OPPORTUNITIES PRESENT THEMSELVES.

Whatever you call it, the point is simply to assemble a group of diverse humans who have your back. And by that I mean diversity in all directions: diverse in cultural background, in thinking, in skill sets. Meet once a week, once a month, once a quarter. Share your experiences, fears, creative ideas, aspirations. Celebrate each other's accomplishments. Challenge and support each other. Discover what you are capable of doing when you combine your collective powers.

Productive Disruption

1. Assemble your legion.
2. Schedule your first meeting.
3. At your meeting, go around the room and have each person respond to the question: *What is your superpower at work?*

ASK FOR A RAISE IN HAIKU

Disclaimer: I'm not promising the following technique will get you a raise. But I'm not promising it won't. However, I did crowdsource it with several hundred Creative Trespassers, and based on their responses, it appears that this exercise works, at the very least as a creative way to blow off steam about being underpaid and/or celebrate your unique value within a job (even when our boss may not seem to be celebrating). And even if it doesn't get you a zero added to your paycheck right away, it WILL get you noticed, and maybe pave the way for a future raise.

A haiku is a Japanese poem that uses five syllables for the first line, seven syllables for the second, and five syllables for the third line, and that generally celebrates the beauty of the natural world. We're gonna put our own twist on that convention and use it to write a poem that celebrates the beauty of what you bring to the workplace. Here's an example:

I've done a great job
She agreed with me, then said
Yes to the request!

Once you've written your haiku, you want to deliver it to your boss in some creative way. Email it to yourself—and cc her—on Employee Appreciation Day. Have the florist write it on the little card that accompanies the flowers or cupcakes (or both) you send him for his work anniversary. Give it to her at the holiday gift exchange along with an empty envelope. Or go the slightly more sincere route and let your boss know (in haiku) that his leadership is part of why you are thriving. Do whatever feels right to you as long as it shows that you've got awesome creative impulses, that you come up with unique ways of addressing everyday challenges, and that you're capable of seeing the value you bring to work. At the end of the day, your value resides in your being uniquely qualified to be YOU.

CHAPTER 11

OUTGROW
ADULTING

> I doubt that the imagination can be
> suppressed. If you truly eradicated it in a child,
> he would grow up to be an eggplant.
> —URSULA K. LE GUIN, *Science Fiction Writer*

A FEW YEARS BACK, just after leaving SMoCA, I remember running into a former colleague at an art opening at the museum who asked me, "Do you like your new job better than you liked this one?" "I like it different," I told her. To which she replied, with a twinge of jealousy in her voice, "I have a feeling you'd like any job you did." And I was like, "Well, yeah, I mean, my whole philosophy is kinda that with a little imagination you can make even the most mundane jobs playful and innovative." And she said, with a not-too-subtle roll of her eyes, "Nah, not me, I'm too smart to make believe."

I walked away thinking: *Wait a second.* It's incredibly smart to make believe! Make-believe is easy to dismiss as stupid kid stuff, but in reality it's a powerful tool that allows you to imagine possibilities, to be playful and breathe energy into your surroundings, to find joy in the face of fear and adversity. Making believe is what lets you access unlimited solutions to work's toughest problems. It's what brings creativity to life. In fact, the smartest grown-ups I know are the ones who still remember how to make believe like a kid.

We are ALL born creative geniuses—free, playful, and imaginative—and then, somewhere along the way, we unlearn our awesomeness. This is good news, though, because if we know there is creative genius hiding somewhere deep inside of us, that means we have the potential to find it. As Creative Trespassers, it's time to reclaim our inner child!

In the sixties, researchers Dr. George Land and Dr. Beth Jarman designed a creativity test intended to help NASA hire the most innovative engineers and scientists. It tested what's called divergent thinking, or the belief that there are unlimited creative solutions to any problem. And because nobody grasps the idea of unlimited possibilities better than kids, Land and Jarman wanted to see what would happen if they gave a bunch of kids the same problem-solving questions (yes, the same ones given to actual rocket scientists at NASA) and encouraged them to come up with as many creative solutions as possible.

What did they find? Out of 1,600 five-year-olds, 98 *percent* tested at the highest possible level: Creative Genius. Five years later, when the same kids, now ten-year-olds, took the same test, only 30 percent scored at Creative Genius level. Then, five years later, when they were fifteen years old, the number dropped to only 12 percent. By the early 1990s, the study had been opened up to thousands of adults. Guess how many of them tested at the Creative Genius level? A measly 2 percent. Land's response to the outcome of this study was succinct but meaningful: "What we have concluded is that non-creative behavior is learned."

So, how the heck did we start learning to suppress our creativity? One word: adulting. *Adulting* essentially means to act in a way that is expected of an adult. If you were to look up the term in Urban Dictionary, you would find such definitions as "to do grown-up things and hold responsibilities," "to carry out one or more of the duties and responsibilities expected of fully developed individuals (paying off that credit card debt, settling beefs without blasting social media, etc.)," and (my personal favorite) what happens "post adolescence when the light in your eyes fades away and dies." What suppresses our creativity isn't being an adult, but being told we have to act "like an adult." Like it's a role we didn't audition for but somehow got, and now the script is lost in the mail and our director is out to lunch, so all we have is a couple of stage directions, a few weird props, and a date for opening night, and we've got to do our best to play the role of a lifetime. So, we do the best we can. We get a "real" job, maybe a mortgage, a hedge trimmer, a minivan, some kitchen gadgets, debt, and pretty soon, "Look, Mom! I'm adulting with no hands!"

The problem with adulting, or the idea of acting a part, of doing and buying stuff that gives an outward appearance of maturity and success, is that we're missing out on the inward stuff that *really* constitutes maturity and success: creativity, imagination, and play. Without these things, being surrounded by the trappings of adulthood will only leave us feeling trapped.

I was once rushing down a crowded sidewalk in Boston, on my way to give a talk at HubSpot's Inbound conference about how to start a marketing revolution, when I heard a little boy screaming bloody murder. Probably the responsible thing to do would have been to stop and call the cops, but this was a chance for me to share the stage with Dan Tyre, someone I looked up to, and there was no way I was going to be late.

The more I walked, though, the louder the screaming got. Eventually, the little boy, who looked to be about seven years old, appeared right in front of me holding his mother's hand and crying like he was experiencing night terrors, only it was during the day. My curiosity piqued, I forgot about the ticking clock and decided to follow the pair for a few blocks, hoping to find out why this little boy was playing out a scene from a bad horror movie in broad daylight.

Then it hit me: The oddly warm weather in Boston that morning and the seemingly brand-new backpack slung over his slumped shoulders suggested that his mother must be dropping him off, very much against his will, for his first day of school. My impulse was to help him, but how? I had no idea, so I started furiously digging in my backpack for . . . something, anything awesomely powerful to help the kid out. And then I found it. I walked up to the boy and said, "Excuse me, are you starting school today?" He smeared his hand across his wet face and gurgled, "Y . . . yes." "Well, then," I said, "I think you're going to need this magical pen." This grabbed his attention. I extended a pretty regular-looking ballpoint pen in his direction. "Now, this pen has magical powers," I explained. "With it, you can write the story of your day, then you can rewrite it any way you'd like. This pen has the power to create entirely new worlds. Do you think you can use a pen like this?"

Fighting back tears, he nodded. "Yes." He slipped his hand out from his mother's grip and unclenched his fist to receive the magical pen. I carefully placed the pen in his open palm and walked away.

Now, you might be thinking, "Why did you lie to that poor kid, you monster?!" Well, hold on a second. I didn't lie to him, I told him the absolute truth. The truth is that that pen *did* have the power to create entirely new worlds. That pen was his portal to the land of make-believe, and in the land of make-believe, we all have magic powers.

As children, we instinctively understand this. Yet, once we become adults, we willfully reject the notion that there is power in playfulness and imagination. The moment you proclaim *I am too smart to make believe* is the moment you give up on your magical powers. But if you are willing to start making believe, you'll find that magic exists all around you. Here are a few ways you can use the power of make-believe to unleash your creative genius at work.

GET YOUR GROOVE ON

It was 9:00 a.m. on a Monday morning. I was walking down the street in downtown Phoenix, curiously watching the few people who still smoked real cigarettes take deep inhales before heading into their offices to start their workday, when I heard it. The unmistakable melody, piped through surprisingly high-quality outdoor speakers, of Montell Jordan's "This Is How We Do It."

Naturally, I followed the lyrics to their point of origin, and just as Montell belted out, "The party is here on the West side," I saw, no lie, on the west side of the street, through the slick sliding glass doors of the Renaissance Hotel, a formation five lines deep of pencil skirts and gray suits dancing in unison; a sea of buttoned-up peeps, gettin' down.

I slipped into the hotel, unnoticed, and watched the dance until the very last shimmy, after which the exhilarated group of sharply dressed professionals exploded into high-fives and smiles all around. Hell, I started high-fiving too. Who wouldn't?

As the dancers dispersed and headed back to work, I was able to track down the man responsible, Jon Erickson, director of sales and marketing (and sweaty dude in the front row of dancers), to find out why this seemingly random act of Creative Trespassing was happening. He looked at me as though I'd asked whether Arizona is hot in the summertime, and replied in a matter-of-fact voice, "This is how we welcome VIP guests."

IF YOU ARE WILLING TO START MAKING BELIEVE, YOU'LL FIND THAT MAGIC EXISTS ALL AROUND YOU.

Can you imagine throwing your hands in the air and waving them from here to they-er as a strategy to impress customers? And that wasn't the first time they had danced to win business. When a group of meeting planners looking for an event space called Jon to say they didn't have time to come inside for a tour of the hotel, so were just gonna drive by, slow down, and take a quick peek at the property, Jon and his team made a play to grab their attention by doing just what they had done that morning: blaring their hip-hop battle cry through the outdoor speakers and dancing in front of the windows. When the planners drove by, they saw the passion and energy of the staff whooping it up and booked an entire block of hotel rooms, sight unseen. As Creative Trespassers, we can always find wacky and unforgettable ways to make people feel welcome.

FIND YOUR POWER AMULET

It's time for us to all quit adulting and start making like smart, curious, and creative kids who just happen to look like grown-ups. This isn't as hard as it seems. When you find that you've lost your passion for dancing at work, when you feel like you've lost the power of make-believe, when you know deep down that you are suppressing your creative genius, all you need to do is find your power amulet and use it.

What is a power amulet, you ask? Your power amulet is any ordinary object that, when in your possession, can unleash the superpowers you already possess to address everyday challenges, like your ability to observe, to care, to inspire, to change, to imagine. Think of how, in the DC comic *Green Lantern*, when Allen Scott and his superhero successors put on their power rings, they could become invisible, create an "energy twin" to double their power, and do a whole bunch of other cool stuff to fight evil in the universe. For a long time, my power amulet was a specific pair of socks that I would literally wash every night after a performance so I could wear them again. That's how much power those suckers brought to me. Then it was a pair of sneakers. Then two pairs of sneakers (don't ask how that one worked). Then a lucky stone I kept in my pocket. Then it was a lucky rabbit's foot (not so lucky for the rabbit). Then it was a striped blazer. Then it was an orange blazer. Then it was two different stones, a gold coin, and . . . you get the idea. It doesn't even have to be a physical object: I used to sing an Erasure song while playing tennis against my rivals in college. The point is that if you believe in the power of make-believe, everything you can wear, stick in your pocket, collect, or play in your head can become magical.

Tennis great Serena Williams has been known to wear the same pair of socks for an entire tournament. And Academy Award–winning actor Benicio del Toro wears a real-life power ring that is partially made out of wood so that, you got it, he can knock on it when he needs a little extra luck. What will your amulet do?

Productive Disruption

1. Choose your power amulet.
2. Carry it with you when you show up on your first day of work, when you give a big presentation, when you have an important meeting with your boss or a client, when you write a proposal.
3. Make believe that that object has the power to make you more imaginative, more energized, more inspired, more confident.
4. Use it to unleash your creative genius.

CHAPTER 12

TURN INTO
THE SKID

> Awakeness is found in our pleasure and our
> pain, our confusion and our wisdom, available
> in each moment of our weird, unfathomable,
> ordinary everyday lives.
>
> —PEMA CHÖDRÖN, *Buddhist Nun and Author*

REMEMBER THAT QUESTION on the driver's license test?

*If you are driving on an icy road and your car starts to skid,
what do you do?*

> *a. Turn in the opposite direction of the skid.*
> *b. Press firmly on the brakes.*
> *c. Turn in the direction of the skid.*

I remember when I was sixteen years old, taking the driver's
test at the DMV. The stakes were high; I'd either walk out of
there with a license or be sentenced to spend the rest of the
school year either a) roller-skating to school or b) hitching rides
with sketchy seniors. Unfortunately, I had no idea what to do in
this skid scenario, so I used my imagination to reconstruct it. My
mental picture looked something like this:

So, I'm in Iceland, cruising around some fjords with Björk. She hits a high note. I'm so moved that I turn to applaud and all of a sudden . . . my car starts to skid out of control! Car parts, bottles, and cutlery fly out the window in slow motion. There is a polar bear about fifty feet in front of the car. What do I do? I want to slam on the brakes to avoid hitting this innocent creature. My brain is yelling at me to turn away from the skid. But that's the wrong answer. The correct answer is: c) Turn INTO the skid.

At work, we often face situations or frustrations that leave us feeling like we're skidding out of control, like when a judgy colleague says, "You can't do that, it's not 'Best Practices,'" or we are told "Sorry, but there's no budget for an innovation lab," or when we receive an email from our boss with the four most ominous words ever strung together, "We need to talk."

In those uncomfortable moments, our brain is screaming at us to slam on the brakes, to throw our hands up and accept defeat. But turning away from the everyday annoyances, frustrations, and challenges is not the answer. Instead of swerving away from the skid, we will barrel into it headfirst!

MAKE RESILIENCE A PERSONAL BEST PRACTICE

On November 8, 2016, millions of Americans stayed up until the wee hours of the morning, glued to their screens as votes were tallied, winners of counties were called, and collective breaths were held. But instead of staying up with the rest of the nation anxiously waiting for a winner of the most nail-biting national election in history to be declared, I went to bed at 9:00 p.m. MST. Why? Because I was to give a companywide talk to the leadership team at the health insurance company Humana the next morning, a talk I had been preparing for months. I needed to be on my game and figured I should get my beauty rest.

The following morning, I woke up to some startling news. My free Hulu subscription had been canceled! Those bastards! Oh, and also Donald J. Trump had just been elected the forty-fifth U.S. president. Now, let's put politics aside and just say that regardless of who you were rooting for, the outcome was utterly unexpected. Even DJT looked like he could barely believe it himself. That morning it felt like the world was suspended in shock and disbelief; an alternate reality seemed to have set in.

Not the best morning to give a keynote. In fact, one could argue that it was the worst morning for a liberal lesbian with a potty mouth to talk to a roomful of buttoned-up executives about—no joke—"Resiliency: How to spring up after being knocked down."

But there was no way out of giving this talk: It had been planned for months, the contract was signed, and executives were poised and ready to listen. Turning away from the skid wasn't an option; the only thing left to do was turn into it. I took a deep breath and began reviewing my notes.

That's when I realized that the topic of my speech was exactly what I needed in order to summon the ability to *give* my speech; what better time for this potty-mouthed lesbian to talk about getting knocked down, getting back up again, and kicking ass than while doing it!

Here's the thing about being knocked down. We can stay down on the ground, spitting and cursing our lot in life, or we can choose to get back up and look our challenges straight in the eye.

It's much easier to kick ass when everything is rosy, but it's infinitely more rewarding to do it when things suck. So next time life has got you down, instead of spitting at the universe, stare your setbacks and obstacles in the face, and make the decision to spring back up!

GRAB LIMITATIONS BY THE CLUTCH

Something I hear—a lot—from people in all industries is that they long to be creative at work but don't get enough support from their managers or bosses. Even companies that *say* they champion creative thinking often aren't coughing up resources for it. Once, after hearing me give a talk at PHX Startup Week, for example, two engineers from American Express approached me and said, "We want to start an innovation lab but don't have the space or buy-in; what do you suggest?"

Have you ever been inspired to start a creative initiative, project, or campaign at your company? And have you ever been told that there isn't enough space, money, resources, or buy-in? Whether your idea was to start an innovation lab, a lecture series, or a book club, nothing crushes the spirit harder than limitations, right? Wrong!

By facing our limitations, we can find unlimited options!

Several years ago, I met an artist named Meg Duguid because I had arranged to see an exhibition she curated. But this exhibition wasn't at a gallery or museum; in the absence of the cash or connections to gain access to an experimental space, she decided to curate the exhibition someplace unusual. The project was called Clutch Gallery, which she described as "a twenty-five-square-inch space in the heart of Meg Duguid's purse." After my initial laughter and delight in the absurdity of curating an art exhibition in a purse, I saw the genius in her gesture. She hadn't let the limitations of the art world stop her from curating. Instead, she had grabbed them by the clutch!

Productive Disruption

1. Start an innovation laboratory in a surprising space.

2. Curate experiments.

3. Invite colleagues to participate and contribute.

"TURN INTO" NERVOUSNESS

Does public speaking freak you out? Cool, you're in the majority. It's on most people's list of top five phobias. And yet most of our jobs require us to speak publicly from time to time, in some form or another. Nothing sucks harder than mustering up enough courage to give a talk, make the presentation or pitch, and then . . . a phone goes off, someone has a coughing fit, your PowerPoint isn't working, your brain goes blank, you start saying "um" over and over again. Does this sound, um, sound, um, familiar?

Many proficient public speakers have no problem giving you the following advice: *Turn nervousness into excitement!* Easy for them to say; they're high-energy extroverts with years of public speaking experience. I prefer the following advice: *Turn into nervousness.* What I mean is, instead of trying to hide or deny your stage fright, use it to connect with your audience.

I once coached an extremely introverted executive director who was terrified of public speaking. She told me, "I know it's part of my job, but I am so scared to speak in front of people, when I get up there, I can't even look at them." I said, "Don't." I advised her to start her speech with her back to the audience, without trying to mask her unsteady breathing, and say into the microphone, "Do you ever feel too nervous to face an audience? Yeah, me too."

BY
FACING OUR LIMITATIONS,
WE CAN
FIND UNLIMITED
OPTIONS!

Whether your fear is public speaking, starting a new job, negotiating a raise, or asking someone out on a date, there's a good chance that at least 80 percent of people identify with the very same anxieties you do. By turning into our nervousness, rather than fighting it, we show our audience that we are honest, imperfect, and human, just like them.

CHAPTER 13

CRASH THE
COMPANY PICNIC

Don't sit down and wait for opportunities to
come . . . get up and make them!

—MADAM C. J. WALKER, *Entrepreneur and Philanthropist*

MY FATHER IS the furthest thing from a "company man" you can
think of. He has never owned a company. He has never worked
for a company. In fact, he rarely enjoys the company of others.
Once, he stole a company car, but that's another story. That's
why, in 1983, when my twin brother and I were twelve years old
and our sister was ten, we were confused to learn that good old
dad was picking us up and taking us to . . . a company picnic.

On the day in question, Dad's 1970 saddle-brown Eldorado
Cadillac coupe glided up to the curb, and at the sound of the
familiar shrill honk (strangely, Dad's car had the same New York
accent as Dad himself), all three of us ran outside, excited for an
adventure with our wild dad!

My brother and sister slipped into the backseat, its torn brown
leather smelling of fast food and lost jobs, held together with
year's-old duct tape fraying at the edges. I managed to push my
way into the front seat, roll down the window, and feel the cool,
dry breeze of possibilities.

"I'm gonna take you kids somewhere very special today," Dad

said, pointlessly adjusting his rearview mirror, which had been broken and repaired so many times that the range of motion was approximately one centimeter to the left or one centimeter to the right.

"To buy a Cabbage Patch doll?" my sister asked optimistically.

"Nah, it's better than cabbage picking," Dad said. "We're going to . . . a company picnic!"

The three of us screamed in unison, "YAY!"

In retrospect, I'm not sure why we were so excited about a company picnic, considering we didn't know what either of those two words—company or picnic—really meant. But if our dad was excited, so were we. Plus, we were ten and twelve, so we didn't really have much else going on that day other than bickering over which cartoons to watch.

We arrived at the park. Dad popped out of the car, grabbed an itchy plaid blanket from the trunk, tucked it under his arm, and said, "Okay, kids, let's go!"

Dad walked fast, with a sense of purpose and urgency usually reserved for when he was getting ready to go to Vegas, and we did our best to keep up with him, our little legs moving as quickly as they could.

Then, in the distance, something caught his eye. "Come on!" he said, and began walking even faster, then broke into a full-on gallop.

Out of breath and theories about where Dad could possibly be taking us, we finally stopped at the foot of a giant blue and white sign that read: WELCOME TO THE MOTOROLA COMPANY PICNIC! Dad stood for a moment, arms akimbo, looking up at the sign with reverence. "Kids, grab a hot dawg and some soda. We're here!"

"Um . . . Dad, you don't work for Motorola," I said, but my Captain Obvious comment came a beat too late, as Dad already had a foot-long hot dog in hand and was excitedly decorating it with a thick mustard zigzag.

Had my father really just crashed a company picnic to score free hot dogs? And worse yet, brought his innocent children along as accomplices? Didn't he have a sense of dignity? Of right versus wrong?

After pondering these existential questions, I closed my eyes and prayed in the only way I knew how at the time. "Dear God, it's me, Tania. Could you please provide me with a new, less embarrassing, more financially stable dad by three p.m. today? That's all. Oh, and maybe a shar-pei puppy. Thanks."

As my eyes opened I saw several fathers happily bouncing down a stretch of grass, holding potato sacks up around their waists. Maybe one of them was my new dad? I looked carefully, and then I saw him: morally inferior actual Dad. My father was potato-sack-racing with the real Motorola employees! Despite the sweat dripping down his face, threatening to expose the mustache he had filled in with mascara earlier that day, he looked oddly strong, almost elegant, like so many of the horses he had bet—and lost—on over the years.

The company men were dropping like flies. But my father showed no signs of slowing down. All those years working as a Manhattan cabbie had apparently paid off; the demanding rock stars in the backseat, the death threats and middle fingers from other drivers, the lingering smell of vomit, the overnight driving, had, it seemed, forged in him a grit and resilience that gave him a leg up on those soft corporate workers.

The field quickly thinned out until only two racers remained: my father and a company man. I could practically hear the sportscaster's play-by-play in my head: Looks like Dad is in the lead . . . Now it's the other guy . . . Now Dad . . . other guy . . . Dad . . . other guy . . . DAD . . . OTHER GUY . . .

The blue ribbon stretched across the finish line practically jumped up to hug my father as he leaned in to win the race. For exactly three seconds I was proud of my father. By the fourth second, I hoped that the smoke from the nearby grill would fill our lungs and kill us both.

I gathered up my brother and sister and went to confront the new potato-sack-race champion, who I found reveling in his victory with a group of company men over some beers. He was telling them a story, cursing and gesticulating wildly like only a guy who didn't work for a company would. Yet these guys were laughing, listening to Dad, the company picnic crasher, like he was not merely a colleague, not just any old employee of Motorola. They were treating him like he was the freaking CEO.

As you can imagine, incidents like the one I have just described were not a rare occurrence. I spent most of my childhood totally embarrassed by my father's penchant for what I've come to call Random Acts of Defiance (not so RAD for me). Don't even get me started on how he snuck me into Girl Scouts without paying dues! Let's just say—THANK GOD—the Girl Scout code of conduct clearly states, "Be friendly and helpful," otherwise those thin-mint-loving green berets would have been within their rights to rip my homemade sash right off of me.

And yet, I learned some key lessons from my father's renegade behavior, ones that have actually (though I'd never admit this to him, of course) contributed to much of the success I've been fortunate enough to have in my career. I know what you're thinking, *Um, Tania, how could your father's sneakery help anyone excel in work, life, or anyplace other than a jail cell?* Fair question, but here's the thing about my dad's funny business. Basically, he was an expert at finding unconventional applications for his pretty conventional skills: something we need to do all the time in the working world. Whether we're pitching a new client or starting a new job or angling for a promotion, we need to be able to assess our skills and understand how and when they can be transferred into different contexts.

In my pop's case, he transferred his skills of scamming, disarming with charm, and disregarding authority into critical thinking, problem solving, and strategic planning that led to hooking him and his kids up with free hot dogs and bragging rights as reigning potato-sack-race champion.

If you're still skeptical that the lessons of a picnic crasher can help you get and stay ahead, maybe you'll be persuaded by this story of how a CEO I once worked with benefited from her aptitude for sneakery. This particular CEO of an arts organization had contacted me to help her relocate her creative mojo. As the new leader of a large operation, she was feeling insecure about leading without having "all the knowledge necessary to lead." As a result, she admitted to me, she'd let her creativity play second fiddle to her leadership, thinking for some reason that playing by the rules would make her look more experienced and leaderly. Instead of trusting her creativity to *guide* her leadership, she was fighting against it.

She had been a creative person her entire life: a writer, theater director, and performer, but when it came to leading an organization, she had allowed her imagination to get swallowed up by an ocean of metrics, data, and budgets . . . Oh my! The problem was, repressing her creative self had left her—and her employees—feeling "uninspired." In working with her to reclaim her creativity, I asked her to make a list of all the sneaky stuff she did as a kid. Then I had her pick one especially sneaky escapade that stuck out. For her, the choice was as clear as Christmas— especially since it happened *on* Christmas.

Even as a toddler, she recounted to me, she had always been curious and resourceful. So by the time she hit the ripe old age of six, she figured out how to parlay her resourcefulness into the one thing that mattered the most to her: getting an early peek at her Christmas presents.

So one snowy December night, she waited until her parents went to sleep, then she stealthily made her way downstairs, grabbed all the shiny gifts sitting under the tree with her name on them, took them back to her bedroom, unwrapped them, took a peek at each one, then carefully rewrapped them and placed them back under the tree as if nothing had ever happened.

I was duly impressed and told her so. But I could tell she still didn't see what her childhood mischief had to do with her current predicament. I then asked her to make a list of all the skills she had drawn upon to execute her Christmas mission. Here's what she came up with:

Observation *(had to see and remember exactly how the gift was wrapped and where it belonged under the tree)*
Speed and agility *(so I wouldn't get caught)*
Risk taking *(because I could have easily gotten caught)*
Public speaking *(had to choose my language carefully and present a compelling story when I opened the gift in front of my parents and they asked how I liked it)*
Curiosity *(because there was something I wanted to know, so I decided to explore it)*

Then I asked her to write down all of the skills she thought someone needed in order to be a successful leader. As if on cue, she listed:

Observation *(ability to see and prioritize programmatic needs and successfully execute goals, objectives, and the mission of the organization)*

Speed and agility *(ability to work in a fast-paced environment under pressure, guiding good ideas, people, processes forward)*

Risk taking *(nurturing a culture of experimentation and creativity)*

Public speaking *(spokesperson for the organization, clearly communicating the mission and vision to all stakeholders while inspiring new engagement)*

Curiosity *(constantly learning and sharing methods for making innovative programs and performances. Facilitating opportunities for employees to pursue learning and sharing too)*

You get the point. And so did she.

Our creative abilities are what sets us apart; they are our greatest differentiator. So why do we keep looking for them in all the same old places? Instead, we need to cast a wider net and look for all the ways we are using our creativity outside of the office — then smuggle those skills into our work. So which creative skills haven't you discovered yet? Which ones have been hiding in mental silos labeled "Childhood Shenanigans"? Think about all the sneaky stuff you did as a kid or teen (or an adult with three children and a mild gambling problem). Did you sneak into the movies? Pilfer from your parents' liquor cabinet? Take the family car for a joyride? Crash a company picnic? Throw a steak knife at your little sister for stealing your poster of Duran Duran? That's cool, I don't judge. Maybe you learned a little something about taking responsibility and 'fessing up to your wrongdoing (before that little snitch tells on you, and Mom grounds you for a month), a critical skill for any leader.

Now, tell the truth, what shenanigans do you leave off of your résumé? What would you never think to include in a cover letter? The wild ideas you took permission to implement and the bold solutions you took permission to try—ones that maybe didn't work out but that lit a spark in you and others, leading to even better ideas and solutions down the line? The mistakes that made you laugh and made you feel free? The times you took breaks from your "real work" to connect with real humans and maybe make someone's day? Whatever your random acts of defiance were, I guarantee you that you can find a way to tap those same skills to infuse a sense of imagination, play, and even sneakery (within the boundaries of the law, and your HR department, of course) into your day-to-day work. And I can guarantee that your doing so will only make you more inspired, more playful, and, yes, a better leader.

OUR CREATIVE ABILITIES ARE WHAT SETS US APART; THEY ARE OUR GREATEST DIFFERENTIATOR.

Productive Disruption

1. Start making a list of all your childhood shenanigans.

2. Think about what skills were involved in them.

3. Tap into those skills to help you get unstuck in your adult work.

PLAY THE LONG CON

My father, as we established earlier, was spectacular at gambling, but much less so at holding down a regular job. In the summer of 1976, however, Dad found a once-in-a-lifetime employment opportunity. He could earn one hundred dollars a day selling steaks door to door, no experience necessary! Despite the fact that this golden opportunity would require him to move from New York all the way to Arizona, Dad jumped at the chance to be an entrepreneur, a disruptor in the world of meat retail. His first day on the job, he hit the ground running, or rather walking, around in the ninety-degree weather selling slabs of beef out of a refrigerated pushcart. The problem was, when he showed up at people's homes and lifted the door of the refrigerated cooler to reveal cuts of red meat rather than ice cream, well . . . You can imagine the disappointment on children's faces. After about three hours during which he sold exactly zero steaks, my father decided to throw in the towel and head to the racetracks, where he made two hundred dollars and promptly quit his new job. When I asked him if he had learned anything from this astonishingly short-lived career experience, he said, "You can have your steak and eat it too, but don't ever try to sell it door to door!"

Okay, so Dad's not exactly a modern-day Confucius, but I have to admit that in this particular aphorism lies some wisdom: Don't say yes to every shiny opportunity that comes your way without thinking through how it factors into your larger goals.

Do you have a tendency to take on tasks, projects, jobs, and positions that have about as much potential to move you closer to your dream career as selling frozen meat door to door in Arizona in the summertime? Be aware of the moments when you are running away from your dreams. It's not always a bad idea to take a risk on a new opportunity, just as long as it's an opportunity that will allow you to develop some skills, relationships, passions, and experiences that will advance—rather than derail—your long-term career goals.

CHAPTER 14

LEVEL UP
YOUR LISTENING

Silence is not the absence of sound. Silence is
the absence of distractions.

—ERNESTO PUJOL, *Performance Artist and*
Social Choreographer

IMAGINE THAT FOR your birthday, you've been given tickets to
a concert. You've never heard classical music performed live before, but you figure this is as good a time as any to start. You
arrive at the concert hall and find your seat among the other
concertgoers. As you settle in, you see that on the slightly raised
stage sits a piano and nothing else. All signs point to this being
a piano recital. After a few minutes, the shuffle of fellow concertgoers trying to find their seats, rustling of programs being
opened and riffled through, and muffled chattering subsides.
The lights dim, signifying the beginning of the performance.
You sit at attention, waiting for the performers to take the
stage. Blackout. The space vibrates; the tension is palpable.

When the lights come on, a gentleman dressed in a suit
takes the stage, sits at the piano, carefully arranges his sheets of
music, retrieves a stopwatch from his pocket, presses a button on
the watch, sits up straight, and looks out into the audience. He
lifts the fallboard, exposing the piano's black and white keys. He

stares down at the keys for a moment, then a moment longer, and another. Then, instead of tickling the ivories, he reaches for the fallboard and quietly closes it. He looks up at the sheets of music, turns the page as if he has just finished a piece and is moving on. He sits quietly for a minute or so, then once again opens the fallboard and looks at the keys without touching them, then turns a few pages of music, closes the fallboard, sits in silence for a few more minutes. He looks at his stopwatch again. Ceremoniously presses "stop." Gets up from the piano and leaves the stage. Four minutes and thirty-three seconds have passed without a note of music, and the performance is over.

What's going on here? you think to yourself. *Is this a joke? Where's the music?*

Okay, first you should know that this composition, called 4'33" (four minutes and thirty-three seconds), was created by avant-garde composer John Cage in the early 1950s. Premiered by pianist and experimental composer David Tudor for a rather stunned audience at the Maverick Concert Hall in Woodstock, New York, on August 29, 1952, the composition has been performed all around the world, by many performers, and to many concertgoers' amusement, shock, and every emotion in between.

Cage is known for his innovative compositions and unusual instruments, which have included electric mixers, a bathtub, Crock-Pots, radios, a quail call, and a live audience. But total silence?? There were surely those in the audience who wondered if perhaps Cage had taken "avant-garde" too far. But 4'33" wasn't a joke or a stunt. What Cage was asking us to do is shift our attention away from the place we expect music to come from (the piano) and open our minds—and ears—to the possibility that, in fact, music is all around us.

Cage believed that *every* sound could be music, it's just a matter of how you listen to it. Music, by definition, is what happens when sounds coalesce to create harmony, discord, emotions, and beauty. So, by his estimation, the coughing, rustling of programs, buzz of stage lights, and chattering of audience members that filled the otherwise silent concert hall for the four minutes and thirty-three seconds of Cage's performance are, in fact, music.

When we actively listen to the world around us, we realize that we are always creating music. Listening reminds us that we are a part of something larger than ourselves. Listening is an art form.

But there is a difference between listening and hearing. Hearing is passively perceiving sounds; it's involuntary; it involves no effort at all. Listening, on the other hand, requires us to be actively engaged in the world around us. Listening demands that we access all of our senses so we can interpret and find meaning in sounds that we are hearing.

My friend Mary Kay once lived on one of the busiest streets in Phoenix, Arizona. Her window overlooked four lanes of traffic that never let up. Like a freeway, only no off-ramps. A veritable symphony of roaring car engines, tires slamming into potholes, eighteen-wheelers bouncing on cracked asphalt, horns blaring, and more played constantly, day and night. One day, when a few friends and I were visiting her, we inquired about how the hell she was able to deal with all of that freaking noise. She said, "I just go to the beach." My initial thought was "She's lost it"—an understandable reaction given that she lived in a landlocked city. Then she grabbed a few plastic lawn chairs, placed them on the sidewalk that abutted the busy street, and asked us to sit down. Then she said, "Close your eyes and listen to the waves." Sure enough, when we actively focused on listening to and reinterpreting the sounds around us, no shit, those cars sounded like waves breaking at dawn! It was incredible. Now, whenever I'm walking on a busy street and long for the stillness and calm of the beach, I close my eyes and listen to the waves.

The blank page, at first glance, can be startling in its silence, its emptiness, its nakedness. But just as the four minutes and thirty-three seconds of silence allowed the audience to truly listen to their own music, the blank page gives us a space to listen to our thoughts, make connections, and let our imaginations run wild.

Often our inclination is to talk through the silence, to doodle on the empty page. When the empty page leaves us paralyzed by fear, or a creative block, sometimes the best thing we can do is put pen to paper and start filling it up. Conversely, when our brains are working a mile a minute and our heads are full of clutter and noise, what we often need most is space to quiet our minds, explore our surroundings, and get out of our own way. Sometimes filling up the space leaves us empty-handed, but listening to the emptiness can fill us with wonder.

THE BLANK PAGE GIVES US A SPACE TO LISTEN TO OUR THOUGHTS, MAKE CONNECTIONS, AND LET OUR IMAGINATIONS RUN WILD.

As Creative Trespassers, we can learn to inhabit the space in between hearing and listening. Because once we get comfortable with shutting our pie holes and actively listening to the music around us, no space is silent, static, or empty. When we do, that space can be filled with car horns, potholes, or concertgoers coughing—or it can be filled with waves, ideas, and orchestras. Here are some ways you can level up your listening and hear the music that exists all around us.

WHEN WE ACTIVELY LISTEN TO THE WORLD AROUND US, WE REALIZE THAT WE ARE ALWAYS CREATING MUSIC. LISTENING REMINDS US THAT WE ARE A PART OF SOMETHING LARGER THAN OURSELVES. LISTENING IS AN ART FORM.

SAY UH-UH TO UH-HUH

Years ago, a colleague was trying to explain a new process to me and midway through her explanation she stopped abruptly and said, "I can't talk to you anymore!" Obviously, I was taken aback and asked her why the heck not. She looked at me with frustration and said, "Because in between every word I say, you say, 'Uh-huh,' like you already know it all!"

Blech. For the first few months after her unsolicited observation I thought, *She sucks!* Even after I left that job and hadn't seen her in months, every once in a while I'd think about that moment, get a pit in my stomach, and think, *She still sucks!* I carried that moment with me for years. Eventually, anger gave way to curiosity. So, I engaged in a social experiment whereby I paid close attention to how I listened when in conversation with others. Turned out, her observation was spot on. My *uh-huhs* weren't just distracting and annoying, they took up all the empty space between speaking and listening—leaving no room for the information to pass through. I immediately got to work on omitting fillers and allowing for more space to listen and learn.

When I'm leading workshops there's an exercise I often give that requires people to work in pairs; one person is the Listener and the other the Talker, then they switch. Ultimately, the two will collaborate on solving a significant problem in the workplace. When I give the instructions, I always start by saying, "Listeners, your job is to listen." This usually evokes laughter, then I'll add, "That means please refrain from saying anything. No *uh-huhs* or *yeahs*. No offering advice. Just listening." Without fail, I'll then observe participants uh-huhing and yeahing their way through the exercise. Also, I'll observe participants catching themselves in these verbal fillers. This exercise really drives home how instinctive it is for us to fill silence, often without even realizing it. And it helps people see how omitting the fillers creates space to let ideas in.

Productive disruption

1. Pick a partner. Ask your partner to talk about something for five minutes.
2. Listen without speaking.
3. Switch roles.
4. Keep trying until both of you complete a full five minutes of real listening—without interrupting and without fillers.

LISTEN TO YOUR BODY

When I first signed up to run a marathon with a friend, we were drunk and convinced that a) it was a good idea to run 26.2 miles despite our lack of prior experience with any sort of long-distance running, and b) at some point in the race, we would almost certainly end up relieving ourselves on someone's front lawn. Fortunately, I learned two things early on: First, you have to run, like, Olympics-fast to crap your pants (so there was no chance of that happening), and second, if you train well and listen to your body, your body listens back, showing up and knowing exactly what to do on race day.

For seven months leading up to the marathon, I ran four days a week without listening to any music while running, just paying attention to the sounds of my breathing, my feet hitting the treadmill, my accelerating heartbeat. Each week, I increased the number of miles I ran: the first week it was 9 miles, the next 15, then 20, then eventually 25 to 28.

By the time my friend and I showed up at the start line and the announcer yelled, "GO!" my body was calling the shots without my brain getting in the way. In order to run that great distance, you can't be thinking about how many more miles you have to go or how many miles you've run. You have to be totally present, in your body, aware of your surroundings. Listening to the needs of your body becomes essential in running long distances. Is it telling me I need more water, a snack? Is it saying I have a blister, a cramp?

For 26.2 miles, I was fully present, my brain completely empty of clutter, and full of wonder. My senses were heightened in a way that I'd only experienced while meditating, writing, or performing (and during one really intense edible moment). When all nonessential thoughts and fears leave your mind, you are left with a wide-open space to discover.

We come to work, every day, with our exquisitely imperfect bodies; bodies that have endured indignities, injuries, maybe even severe injuries—and yet they are all poised and powerful in their own ways. Those of us who perform using our bodies—actors, dancers, performance artists, athletes—understand that our body is our "instrument." And the sooner we become aware of all the unique ways in which our body works, the sooner we can be in harmony with it. This is why performers and athletes train, rehearse, practice: so that when the pressure is on, our instincts kick in and our muscle memory does the rest. Like a soccer goalie instinctively blocking the ball from whooshing into the net, when our bodies, minds, and intentions are totally aligned, we are able to respond with clarity and lightning speed to any challenge, situation, or opportunity that comes our way.

In the chaos and noise that often underscore our lives, it becomes essential for us to breathe, stay present, and listen to our bodies. How will *you* listen to your instrument today? Even if the only dancing you're doing is tapping your toes to smooth jazz as you ascend in the elevator to your office on the eighteenth floor, listening to your body will help find the mental calm, focus, and space for creativity to flourish. It will let you know when you need more sleep, more exercise, more fresh air to be fully energized and engaged in work, in play, and in the world.

MAKE THE INVISIBLE VISIBLE

There are a ton of artists, writers, and creatives of all stripes who explore the eloquence of omission, who have spent their lives working to make the invisible visible. Their goal is to show us that the stuff left out of the frame, out of the picture, out of the narrative, is just as important as what our eyes actually do see. Here are just a few examples.

In the mid-eighties, Ilya and Emilia Kabakov created an art installation called *The Man Who Flew into Space from His Apartment.* As you entered the gallery, you would have encountered a boarded-up entrance with enough gaps in between the slats to peer into the space, which held an oppressively cramped one-room apartment. That's when you would have seen the ramblings of a mad scientist lining the walls: layers of drawings sketched by hand, mostly crude studies of outer space with calculations of time, distance, and dates scribbled in the margins. *Clearly,* you'd say to yourself, *I've entered the apartment of someone obsessed with the science of space travel.* On the floor you would see chunks of Sheetrock imperfectly scattered. Then an intense light streaming into the space would draw your attention to the low ceiling. That's when you would notice the huge hole blown out, and underneath it a pair of empty shoes and a contraption that looked like a human-scale slingshot.

Even though you never *saw* the man fly into space from his apartment, you know he did. You don't *need* to see the moment when he took flight, you just need your imagination and enough empty space to let the invisible reveal itself.

Gordon Matta-Clark was an artist who was known mostly for his large-scale architectural interventions called "anarchitecture." He would buy buildings that were going to be destroyed, and literally saw them in half or bore holes into them, allowing the light to come in. His goal wasn't just to give these dying buildings a new life, but to create a new way of making spaces that had once gone completely unnoticed become suddenly visible to the average passerby.

One of his lesser-known interventions quite literally involved transforming "the space between" into artistic creations. He purchased small slivers of land between buildings and houses that went largely unused and unnoticed because they were too small to build on or park a car in (in some cases barely big enough for Matta-Clark to fit his whole body in) and turned them into performance spaces.

He saw the possibilities in these quieter spaces, the ones we ignore or don't even register because they aren't screaming for our attention. When it comes to creativity, sometimes the most expansive spaces are the tiny invisible ones we walk past every single day.

Productive Disruption

1. Find the quieter spaces that exist in between the
screaming ones:

> **Between** home and work.
>
> **Between** you and the person standing across from
> you.
>
> **Between** hearing and listening.

2. Spend some time occupying these invisible spaces, and
allow your mind to wander.

CHAPTER 15

RESUSCITATE
YOUR WORK CULTURE,
FOR ART'S SAKE

Culture is the widening of the mind and of the
spirit.

—JAWAHARLAL NEHRU, *First Prime Minister of India*

WE'RE AT A CAFÉ, me and the SVP of information systems for
a global tech company; I'm picking at a croissant, he's picking
my brain. The company needs some help solving an unexpected
problem, so they've enlisted just about the last person you'd expect them to call as a consultant: me.

The company is big (multibillion-dollar) and scaling fast.
Cool, right? Well, here's the problem: The faster they grow, the
faster they lose their disruptive spirit, the special sauce that made
them so valuable and vibrant in the first place.

SVP asks, "How do we ensure that our teams continue to
take risks and create disruptive technology as we scale?"

I counter with, "Do you currently have any disruptive procedures, processes, or employee engagement opportunities inside
the company?"

"No," he replies.

"Well, then . . ." I say. "Get some disruptive processes in
place. Then hire artists."

SVP laughs.

I wasn't kidding.

His problem was extraordinarily clear: a disconnect between thought and form. I explained that the secret to solving this problem—and most problems—can be found in the way that artists think. Artists are trained to find the connective tissue between thought and form, between the idea and the shape it takes.

Artists are also masters at the art of questioning. By looking at the world through inquisitive eyes, artists can help us break free of entrenched assumptions, mindsets, and processes. As Steven J. Tepper, dean of the Herberger Institute for Design and the Arts at Arizona State University (and a leading writer on U.S. cultural policy as it relates to cultural engagement and creativity in work and careers), explains it: "Routines become very powerful in shaping corporate culture and thinking. They are comfortable grooves that can keep us stuck when, in fact, we need to expand our imagination, test ideas, and work through ambiguity. Artists are trained to live in this ambiguous space. To avoid routine (even while adhering to certain mastery), artists ask "what if" questions. They are imagination partners. Without artists and creatives, corporations will be hostage to their own routines."

If we want innovations to emerge from our companies, we have to create innovative cultures, which means we need strategies for disrupting the same ol' business-as-usual business model. And nobody knows how to get out of a rut, get their groove on, and sustain long-term innovation better than artists! Now, you yourself don't need to be an artist in the traditional sense—a painter, a performer, a writer—to come up with innovative and disruptive solutions to business problems. But it sure as hell helps to surround yourself with a whole bunch of them. And, if you're reading this book, I'm guessing there's already a little bit (to a lot) of artist in you, waiting to break free.

If you want to shake up the culture in your company, team, or workplace, instead of heading to the same dried-up talent pool looking for some sign of life, you gotta go where the real creatives dwell. Finding these people isn't as hard as you think; you've been plotting a map toward them for years. If the ads you're placing on LinkedIn, Indeed, Glassdoor, or anywhere else say things like: "We only hire rock stars!" and "Are you a storyteller who can manage projects?" or "Do you embrace challenges and new methods of thinking with vigor?" or "We are looking for critical thinkers," you're already halfway there.

The other half is to put your money where your mouth is and let your own words lead you to the talent you are truly looking for. You want "rock stars," you're gonna have to go to rock concerts. Keen on storytellers? Head to the theater. Critical thinking and open-mindedness are your company's jam? Go hang out at spoken-word performances or contemporary art museums. To find creative people, you're gonna have to get creative. This chapter is about how.

INVITE INSIGHTS FROM OUTSIDE

I've had the great privilege of speaking at and leading workshops inside of some of the most kick-ass, innovative companies of our time. We're talking Etsy, Carbon, Moz, and more. These companies understand the value in connecting thought and form, so they've created speaker series, conferences, lunch-and-learns, and in-house universities to connect their vibrant employees with more creative learning opportunities and ideas from outside of the company.

These aren't just lame PR ploys or HR initiatives; they are fertile grounds for ideas to cross-pollinate, intellectual curiosity to develop, and insights to emerge. Some of these companies have brought in people like soccer star Mia Hamm, internet trailblazer Ben Silbermann, media impresario Arianna Huffington, author and media theorist Douglas Rushkoff, creativity aficionado Kari Chapin, and so many more disruptors in their respective fields to share their diverse insights, experiences, and ways of thinking about the world. These companies know the value of bringing outsiders inside their culture to help keep people inspired, nudge them out of their mental ruts, and help them chart new paths from idea to action.

Productive Disruption

1. Start a speaker series, a lunch-and-learn, or a user conference.
2. Invite speakers and participants from as many diverse fields as possible.
3. Embrace those outsiders' insights.
4. Use them to spark new innovations inside your organization (and your mind).

RECRUIT OUT OF THE BOX

One of the most brilliant marriages of thought and form I've ever seen was Ikea Australia's employee recruitment campaign. Ikea had a new store opening in Australia, and they needed to hire a lot of employees, superfast. So, with the help of their advertising agency, the Monkeys, they came up with a plan for recruiting, quite literally, "out of the box." They wrote up instructions telling people how to assemble their careers—including how to apply for a job at Ikea—and in true Ikea form, they had those instructions printed and stuffed into boxes, and delivered to customers. Ikea's hiring team figured that the type of person who would follow career advice they stumbled upon while unpacking their furniture was just the type of outsider they needed to shake up the culture. And they were right; in no time at all they were flooded with over four thousand creative applicants and made over two hundred new hires.

WANNA HIRE ROCK STARS? GO TO ROCK CONCERTS!

For most of us the word corporate doesn't exactly conjure associations of punk rock. In fact, for many creative types, it has become a dirty word synonymous with descriptors like soul-numbing, oppressive, greedy, and The Man (and that's the nice stuff). You can almost see the stock photo of corporate, right? A bunch of uptight, suit-clad cats standing in front of a skyscraper, smiling, holding their thumbs up in the air as if to say, "I hate my job, but I still have my thumb, so that's good!" So, you can imagine my surprise when I found out that a VP for a humongous Fortune 500 company is a real-life rock star.

Turns out, Ryan's rocker pedigree has served him well as VP of real estate at one of the biggest retail chains in the country: His years of dodging beer bottles in crappy dive bars and rocking venues with thousands of mohawks and pierced cheeks in the audience was the perfect preparation for his current role leading negotiations with developers and landlords.

Now, as an executive, when he has to give a talk or presentation, he approaches it like playing a gig. "I see myself as an entertainer who needs to engage the audience and be compelling enough for people to want to listen," he says. "Being onstage as a musician prepped me to be behind a podium at a corporate event."

But his rock star training taught him more than just how to

woo an audience. He also had to learn to be resourceful, a skill he draws on constantly in his day job. In the nineties punk scene, no one had managers or agents or marketing consultants; if you wanted to start a band, go on a tour, record, sell T-shirts, book a show, you had no choice but to DIY. "Being in bands forced me to develop business skills early on," he explains. "I was booking shows and tours, managing money, building relationships with promoters and record labels, etcetera. I still carry this DIY attitude to this day, it's how I've been able to grow my career."

Ryan also learned the value of diversity in the workforce through the punk indie scene. "I wasn't one of the kids who played sports or fit in with the popular crowd or had money. In the punk scene, it didn't matter who you were—race, gender, sexuality, appearance, income; the music was the common thread that brought people together. Diversity made the scene stronger and the music better. As I build my teams in a corporate culture now, I still see the value in diversity. Working in a homogeneous environment is both boring and less productive. Diversity brings you a better work product!"

Productive Disruption

1. As a team-building activity, go to a play, dance performance, museum, or concert.
2. Learn from the creative process you observed.
3. Discuss how best to apply these insights to your specific work.

   Bonus: Invite the playwright, choreographer, artist, or composer back to your office, and find threads that connect their work with your business goals. When you find three threads or more . . . Hire.

So, if you're looking to hire a rock star employee with "management experience" and an "entrepreneurial spirit" who is great at "public speaking" and can "represent the company at conferences," maybe it's time to go out and hire a flesh-and-blood rock star. After all, every rock star company needs a punk rocker!

STOP LOOKING FOR PERFECT MATCHES AND START DISCOVERING SLASHES

There was a time in my professional life when my résumé was bursting with creative endeavors and thin in the business-y stuff. Even when I was lucky enough to get an interview with a traditional company, the interviewer, without fail, would say something like: *Well, looks like you're artsy . . . But you haven't worked nine to five, is that going to be hard for you?* And I would politely say, "No."

But what I really wanted to say was: "Hell, no! I work nine to nine, and weekends too! That's what artists do. We don't leave our ideas on the desk until Monday, hoping that they will incubate themselves. We are our own content creators, marketing department, accountants, sales team, front-desk staff, intern, facilities manager, and sandwich delivery service—and we *all* work overtime! And guess what? Sometimes, none of those jobs provides a livable income so we gotta go out and get a slash mark too! By that I mean barista/playwright, research assistant/actor, engineer/novelist, accountant/dancer, office manager/singer, CEO/comedian. Artists have been working multiple gigs at a time long before sleek business publications were even talking about "How to Start a Side Hustle." Nine to five? Puh-lease. That's like a paid vacation!

Whew! Thank you for letting me get that off my chest. The point of this rant? For those of you in a position to hire, please consider relinquishing the Tinder style of hiring: *You have an*

MBA, we need someone with an MBA: swipe left, it's a match! Instead of looking for perfect matches, try to find mismatches that make sense. Inquire about prospective employees' slash marks and side hustles; maybe a data analyst who sidelines as a video game designer, or a publicist who also writes screenplays will be just what you need to take your team or company to the next level. Sometimes the best fit might seem unfit on paper but in real life is the creative nine-to-fiver you're looking for. Consider giving the outsiders, the misfits, the side hustlers, and the artists a chance.

LET YOUR COOL AUNT TELL 'EM!

When I'm leading trainings or speaking, lemme tell you, people listen. Not because I have a tendency to get all loud and jump up and down like a blissed-out Energizer Bunny when I give talks (though that's sometimes true), not because their boss told them it's mandatory or because they think there's going to be a quiz later. They listen because I don't work with them day after day. Even when I'm spouting out some pretty challenging stuff, or when I'm basically saying, "If you don't change your mindset ASAP, you're never going to see the creative, collaborative results you want," those folks are still leaning forward, eager to hear it like it is, smiling. Sometimes they even thank me for it! Mind you, what I'm saying could be the same thing that a colleague or manager might have said a million times, but that's exactly the point: It is infinitely easier to receive a big fat reality check from someone you don't work with. It's the difference between your office mate telling you, "If you don't embrace change, you're gonna get left behind" and your supercool aunt saying, "You don't like change? That's not cool, let's smoke a joint and chitty-chat about it while cruising in my 1970 Corvette Stingray convertible."

When companies desperately need a creative shot in the arm but have no idea where to find a clean needle, hiring a consultant, coach, or trainer is often a good option. And totally legal!

CONSIDER GIVING THE OUTSIDERS, THE MISFITS, THE SIDE HUSTLERS, AND THE ARTISTS A CHANCE.

CHAPTER 16

FIRE
HIERARCHY

> To be truly visionary we have to root our
> imagination in our concrete reality while
> simultaneously imagining possibilities beyond
> that reality.
>
> —bell hooks, *Cultural Critic and Writer*

SO, I'M THIRTY-FIVE thousand feet in the air when the spunky flight attendant taps me on the shoulder, smiles, and says, "Watch this." She grabs the microphone and with a gleam in her eye instructs everyone in the cabin to turn to the right-hand bank of windows and stare out into the sky. "Do you see it?" she asks into the mic.

The flight attendant pauses for a moment, then grabs the microphone again and says, "If you missed it, turn to your left." This time, the passengers crane their necks urgently, clamoring to see whatever they missed the first time around.

One by one, the passengers survey the sky, determine they've missed "it" again, and return to their naps, books, and electronic devices. That's when the flight attendant taps me on the shoulder and says, "We're on an airplane flying five hundred miles per hour . . . we're not flying in a circle, duh!"

Turns out, there was nothing to see out that window at all. The flight attendant was just having some fun and in the process demonstrating something that philosophers have taken lifetimes trying to prove: All human beings fall into one of two buckets: either we are one of the masses following inane instructions, or we are grabbing the microphone giving the instructions.

Upon closer examination, I realized that what she had done was subversive in other ways too. Usually it's the pilot who grabs the microphone and points out the mountain ranges and glacial formations. It's the pilot who makes funny, muffled jokes; it's the pilot who announces that we are stuck on the runway or warns us of upcoming turbulence. Usually, the pilot is the lead singer, and the flight attendants are the backup chorus. But this flight attendant had shown us that you don't need to be the one wearing the stripes to wake people up, make a joke, or pick up the mic and take charge.

This strange incident reminded me of a brain-teaser question a friend in high school once asked me. *Who is more important, a surgeon or a car mechanic?* Then, after a beat, she added an important detail: *When your car is broken down.* The point is that no one's skills are objectively more valuable or important than anyone else's. What matters—as with most things—is context.

In the workforce, we all have unique skills and talents. And no matter what your rank or title is, there will be times when your skills are more valuable and times when they will be less valuable, depending on the task or challenge at hand. Depending on the context and the needs of the team or organization, sometimes you'll be the surgeon and other times the mechanic.

Maybe a pipe leaks in the office building and it's the maintenance worker whose skills become most important. Or maybe the CEO is struggling to improve the company's social media footprint, and it's the Instagram-savvy marketing intern with the right skills to help him out.

There is nothing like a corporate hierarchy to choke the life right out of an idea. Am I right? Oh, you need to ask a decision maker first. Okay, I'll wait. What, you have to ask another decision maker? And another? A work culture in which every idea has to make its way past every single decision maker is a work culture in which nothing gets done. And if you think that all flat organizations have decision making figured out, think again. I worked at one flat org, and lemme tell you about the painstaking hours and days it took to make one teeny decision because nobody wanted to step on anyone's toes until finally the CEO would just swoop in and make the decision for us. This was a hierarchy cloaked as a flat org, and it made decision making as efficient as trying to capture a unicorn with pimento loaf! And let's not forget that CEOs always have to be cognizant of the quarterly numbers, share prices, and payroll before deciding to take creative risks. Often, it's the people with less responsibility and a less flashy job title—or in other words, the people with less to lose—who have the greatest capacity to decide to be boldly creative.

If you're willing to subvert traditional hierarchy, you'll be on your way to breaking down barriers between people, fostering more connection and collaboration, and creating fertile ground for ideas to take root and blossom. We're so quick to assign people labels in the workplace—these people are "the creatives," these people are the "decision makers," these people are the behind-the-scenes support staff whose role is to be "seen but not heard." A culture that assigns such labels is one where creativity dies on the vine because people are afraid of violating their assigned roles, or speaking out of turn, or expressing an idea that might help the company because it falls outside their specific job function.

If you ask me, many companies could stand to take a page from the Fluxus art movement of the 1960s. Just as every industry has its rules, regulations, and hierarchy, so does the art industry. Museums and galleries are often anointed as the gatekeepers of artists, responsible for choosing, grooming, and inviting those special few to grace a gallery wall with their work. The Fluxus artists kicked that hierarchy to the curb and created sets of instructions to inspire anyone and everyone to make and experience art anywhere, at any time. Borrowing from the world of music, the Fluxus artists called their works "scores," because they were meant to encourage people to conduct their own experiences and stage their own performances.

Here is one from Fluxus artist George Brecht:

Exercise
Determine the limits of an object or event.
Determine the limits more precisely.
Repeat, until further precision is impossible.

(To read more scores by Fluxus artists like Yoko Ono, Geoffrey Hendricks, Alison Knowles, Nam June Paik, and more, check out the Recommended Resources listed at the end of the book.) The following score was inspired by Brecht's and made in honor of one of my all-time fave restaurants, whose owners realized that the people washing dishes deserved to own a home just as much as the managers of the restaurant, so they decided to pay everyone the exact same wage!

See the steady stream of dirty dishes
Watch the steady stream of dissatisfied customers

Determine which employees are more important than others
Determine which employees deserve to own a home
Calibrate salaries accordingly

Both in the business of art, and in the art of business, creativity requires cracking the veneer of self-importance, recognizing people's unique abilities, and giving everyone permission to come on board and grab the mic.

GIVE AN OFFICIAL/UNOFFICIAL AWARD

Leadership isn't a position you can attain by simply climbing the metaphorical ladder. It's not about fame or glory or ownership. Being a leader lies in the being. We don't have to be officially in charge to lead; leadership is something that already exists within us and something we already do (or can do) every day. If you go to work and are supportive, empathic, creative, communicative, and even a little inspirational, then you're already leading!

The problem is that many companies don't sufficiently acknowledge those everyday leaders who lighten up a meeting with a joke, add unexpected depth to collaborations, send get-well-soon cards to colleagues who are sick, or champion diversity and inclusion in the workforce. They give out awards like Employee of the Month, Best Sales Performance, and so on, but what about those awesome folks who contribute arguably more through their creativity, empathy, and support? Why can't they get an award? Well, as unofficial leaders . . . we can give it to them! We don't have to put an official logo on it and wait for marketing to review the copy, HR to approve it, and an all-hands meeting to deliberate over it. Why wait for someone on the official leadership team to acknowledge the awesome humans doing inspiring stuff every single day?

Productive Disruption

1. Decide on the awardee.

2. Come up with a title for the award.

3. Present the award to the awardee.

4. Repeat (often).

This award can go to anyone in your office who does not have an official leadership title but who frequently inspires others with his or her kindness, playfulness, or creativity. Once you have figured out what to call your award, cut it out of construction paper, sew it on a tea towel, email it, sneak into the recipient's office and make it the person's screensaver, or simply print it out and present it to the deserving awardee.

I'd like to present you with the . . . Inclusionary Visionary Award . . . You Make Meetings Fun Award . . . Imagination Partner Gold Medal! This award comes with a firm handshake, eye contact, a smile, deep appreciation, and a certificate made out of envelopes I stole from the supply cabinet . . . cuz you're worth it!

Once you start doing this, you might find that you begin seeing more award winners everywhere you go. The barista who is always patient with you as you struggle to decide on soy or almond milk while the customers behind you get increasingly grumpy. The cook at your child's school who sneaks veggies in from her garden to make sure the kids are getting their vitamin C. The bus driver who always waits for you when he sees you sprinting down the block. Or anyone else who takes extra care to improve other people's lives in ways big and small: that's leadership.

CREATIVITY REQUIRES GIVING EVERYONE PERMISSION TO COME ON BOARD AND GRAB THE MIC.

STICK IT TO THE MAN AND WOMAN!

I don't think there's a workplace on the planet that doesn't have a lifetime supply of sticky notes lying around in a supply closet somewhere. Sticky notes are like the Creative Trespassers of paper. They're brightly colored, and their purpose is to stand out and draw attention to stuff we might overlook. And they even have adhesive.

Many moons ago (the 1980s) in an office far, far away, before there was direct deposit (I know, just close your eyes and try to imagine), when all employees received their paychecks IRL, in the form of an actual, physical check, there was a Creative Trespasser named Dan Tyre who used to stick sticky notes onto everyone's paychecks. As the founder and CEO of the company, he would intercept the checks before they were delivered, and to each one he would attach a Post-it on which he'd written a motivational message or words of praise and encouragement. To this day, the recipients of his sticky notes remember receiving their checks and being excited to find a personalized message reminding them that they were seen, valued, and supported.

Unfortunately, the norm in most companies dictates that praise be relegated to HR-sanctioned intervals or reserved for when someone does something extraordinary. But Dan understood the value of disrupting these arbitrary rules for when praise could be permitted—and of showing appreciation for the dedication and passion his employees brought to work every day. After all, they don't call work a grind because it's easy, and sometimes the difference between staying at a job and sweating it out or leaving is being seen, valued, and supported along the way.

PUT THE *CO-* BACK INTO COLLABORATION

When I was in college, I took a class called Theater Collaboration taught by celebrated theater director Marshall W. Mason. In attendance were five playwrights, five directors, and twenty actors. Our assignment: One playwright and one director (selected randomly) would partner with four actors to come up with an idea for a ten-minute play and, with everyone's input, write it and perform it in class. Well, it didn't take much time for us playwrights to get irritated with the actors who had the gall to think they could write, and for the directors to watch their carefully orchestrated blocking be thrown out the window by the actors, and for the actors to insist that no one was listening to their ideas. This led to intense debates about which discipline was the most important in the collaborative process. We playwrights thought, of course, that we were the most important because without a script, there is no play, duh. But the actors argued that without them, the script is just a pile of pages.

Without a director, the directors among us pointed out, there is chaos. Without a set designer there is nothing to anchor us in a place and time, and without the stage manager nothing gets done and you have to bring your own snacks! Pretty quickly, we realized that if we were going to make it through this class, we would have to let go of our perceived pecking order and put the *co-* back into collaboration.

Theater, by design, is a nonhierarchical pursuit. It only works when all the elements come together; if just one is missing or sticking out, the entire operation falls apart. We go to theater (or any live performance) to be moved in some way, to laugh in the dark, to cry with our fellow humans, to *feel* something. But when any one person onstage or backstage pulls rank, demanding to be heard over all the others, that's when we stop feeling and start seeing the flaws in it all.

This is just as true in the workplace as it is onstage. Instead of bailing out on your part or grabbing the spotlight and trying to steal the show, we need to practice co-creating, allowing *the work* to be the star.

LEAD A TEN-MINUTE CREATIVE REVOLUTION

I once worked with a guy who often took it upon himself to run around the office once a day screaming at the top of his enthusiastic lungs, "Movement session!" And for ten glorious minutes, those who wished to drop everything and move their bodies would gather in the middle of the office building, where he led us in a movement session—everything from stretches to jumping jacks. It was sheer bliss. But here's the thing: Nobody gave my coworker permission to do this; he just took it. And who could complain? We didn't lose any clients, we didn't lose time in our day to execute on important projects, we didn't lose focus. In fact, we gained energy and flexibility and regained a sense of playfulness that carried into the work we did. The point is, anyone can make a decision to lead a creative revolution for ten minutes every day.

Productive Disruption

1. Enlist a few fellow Creative Trespassers from your office and take turns leading creative ten-minute breaks.
2. Each day, one leader decides on the form and the prompt for that day's break.
3. Examples:
   a. Writing, nonstop, and the prompt is: What is the story of your name . . . Go!
   b. Drawing, nonstop, and the prompt is: Your first pet . . . Go!
   c. Dancing, nonstop, in the style of hip-hop, ballroom, break dancing, tap, or twerk . . . Go!

CHAPTER 17

REFRAME
THE BLAME

> When you plant lettuce, if it does not grow well,
> you don't blame the lettuce.
>
> —THICH NHAT HANH, *Peace Activist*

THERE WAS A TIME in my professional life when—though I don't mean to brag—I was the king, queen, and the freaking court jester of Blameville. I was practically virtuosic in finding someone else to hold responsible for things that went wrong in my career.

But hey, none of it was my fault! It was my mom's fault, because she encouraged my individuality and never taught me how to play well with the other kids in the sandbox. It was my dad's fault because the only consistent work he ever had was gambling: not the best role model for learning how to take responsibility for one's actions. It was my boss's fault for being such a jerkface. It was the never-ending workload. It was the uninspiring work culture. It was the new person they hired; I just didn't like his attitude. And none of my co-workers listened to my really great ideas. My desk chair was so uncomfortable, I couldn't get anything done. I didn't even have a team! Then, when I got a team, they were totally unsupportive. In fact, the whole company kind of sucked. I had to work late. No one responded to my emails.

The systems were slow and inefficient. The work was so boring I couldn't possibly be expected to be creative. I didn't get paid as much as I was worth. So I showed them and only did the bare minimum amount of fairly mediocre work. They had it coming. They were keeping me stuck.

Turns out, however, that the only person that was really keeping me stuck was lil' old me. But the moment I decided to take responsibility for my work-life misery was the moment I took back the power to change my fate. Truth be told, there's something very comforting in the realization that we don't have any control over most things in life. But what we *do* have control over is whether we let go of the blame or let it consume us.

Once, during a therapy session, my therapist held open her hand, palm up, and said, "This is letting go." Then, she flipped her hand over, palm facing down, and said, "This is giving up." The point was: the difference between letting go and giving up is just the flick of a wrist. It's a simple choice, yet one equals freedom and the other equals staying stuck.

You don't need to see a mental health professional in order to reclaim your personal freedom (though if you have health insurance, I highly recommend it; therapy rocks). This chapter is your chance to get over all the blaming and complaining without the co-pay.

Of course, in many cases—when our chairs are uncomfortable, colleagues aren't responding to emails, and we aren't being paid what we're worth—it isn't completely our fault. But instead of blaming, we can hold people—and organizations—accountable by speaking up about what we need and standing up for what we deserve. There is a difference between blaming and holding accountable: Accountability has a beginning, middle, and end, whereas blame springs eternal. Time to cut off blame at its source. Because when the well of excuses runs dry, that's when we can experience a wellspring of creativity!

Productive Disruption

1. Take out a sheet of paper and list all the unfair, unjust, un-effing believable crap slung at you between the hours of nine and five.
2. Write down all the reasons why it's someone else's damn fault that you are unhappy, unconfident, and unimaginative at work.
3. Now escort that list to the nearest bonfire, shredder, or trash can.

IF YOU'RE BORED, YOU'RE BORING

Whenever her children would complain, "There's nothing to do around here. I'm so bored!" my mother-in-law would reply, "Then you must be boring. Only boring people get bored." Sounds a little harsh, but those three kids grew up to become an internationally recognized artist, a founder and CEO of an expedition company, and the founder of a global nonprofit that improves the lives of children living in poverty around the world. And I can't help but think their success owes a lot to having been taught that boredom is a choice. Instead of letting her kids sit back and wait for the world to wake them up, my mother-in-law encouraged them to wake up to the world around them: to read, to play, to think, and to explore.

I've used this strategy quite successfully in my coaching. A client I once worked with was burned out at work. The parts of her job that used to bring her a sense of joy and fulfillment now felt like a growing list of irritants. She questioned whether she needed a new job or a new life, or both. When I asked her *why* she was so unhappy at her job, she shrugged her shoulders deject-edly and said, "I'm just bored." And so I replied, without missing a beat, "Then you must be boring."

At first she seemed quite taken aback, as though someone with much more upper-body strength than I have had slapped her across the face. But once she regained her composure she looked me straight in the eye and admitted, "I am boring. That's the problem."

WHEN THE WELL OF EXCUSES RUNS DRY, THAT'S WHEN WE CAN EXPERIENCE A WELLSPRING OF CREATIVITY!

Pshaw! Boring is not a genetic trait like height or eye color; it's a learned behavior. This woman wasn't born boring, it's just that she had been stretching her "not interested" muscle for so long that her "totally interested muscle" was starting to atrophy. She didn't need a new job or a new life; she needed to practice being interested and engaged to build back her professional strength.

In theater, we often perform the exact same show five nights a week and twice on Sundays. And, if we're lucky, we'll perform that same show seven times a week for months and sometimes even years. People outside of the theater community are always saying to me, "Doing the same show over and over again has got to be so boring! I could NEVER do that." To which I always reply, "Guess what? You already do it."

The truth is that whether you're sitting at your desk from nine to five or standing on a stage from seven to nine, you're performing the same show over and over. The only difference is that in theater, once the lines are memorized and the blocking learned, we know it's our job to find something fresh, new, and unexpected to bring to our performance every single night. We know that the energy we bring to the stage each night is always different, just as the energy of an audience is always different, which means that we can bring the same show, the same lines, the same dialogue to life in a unique way, night after night. One night we're delivering a joke and at that exact moment a baby in the audience starts crying and everyone misses the punch line. One night we deliver a line meant to evoke tears and the audience erupts in laughter. One night we've just gotten out of a soul-sucking relationship and bring that energy to our performance, and the play takes on a whole new meaning altogether. Performing is the opposite of boring because it dares us to find new ways to cope with, inhabit, and find newness in the unfolding world around us.

What most people don't realize is that work is also a live performance. Every day most people show up to the same office at the same time; we play the same role, we interact with the same characters, we perform the same functions. But the energy we exchange with our coworkers, the way we deliver an email, pitch, or product, how we deal with the challenges that unfold in front of us—that all changes, every day. Every performance is profoundly different. Every performance is a chance to see, experience, and learn something new. When you approach your work that way, it's almost impossible to be bored—or boring—no matter what type of work you do.

Productive Disruption

1. Try going into work tomorrow as if it were your first day on the job. Bring all of that day-one curiosity with you.
2. Allow procedures and tasks to absorb you (rather than bore you) as they did when you were learning them for the first time. Look at your familiar colleagues with fresh eyes.
3. Reconnect with the reasons why you chose this job, because you *did* choose it. Do this exercise for a week, a month, a year. Every day, search for something new and thrilling about the work you choose to do.

Bringing a sense of curiosity and wonder to the office each day won't only make you more interesting; it will make you more creative, more engaged, more inspired. What a gift to you and your employers. So take my mother-in-law's advice: Stop complaining that you're bored and go rediscover something interesting in your work.

ENGAGE IN FUNNY BUSINESS

My mother has been using humor to reframe the blame since back when she worked as a drug and alcohol counselor in a town with some of the most extreme methamphetamine use in the United States. She worked with serious addicts, repeat offenders, and people that many counselors didn't want to work with. Instead of blaming her patients for their self-destructive behavior, my mother used humor to reframe the situation by coming up with her own private nickname for this drug-infested town: "I call it our Little Town of Methlehem!"

And when the patients in her therapy group became disillusioned by the long road to recovery (not to mention the fact that most of them couldn't even drive on that road because their driver's licenses had either been suspended or taken away altogether), my mom used her good humor to reframe the situation by holding a bumper sticker contest for the group. Everyone delighted in coming up with original sayings like "Honk if you love prison tamales!" and "My other car is in my drug dealer's driveway" and "I love my Chevrolegs!" My mom came up with one too: "Take the high road, but don't take the road high!"

My mother's skill at reframing even extended to aphorisms. When my siblings and I were little and came home repeating sayings we heard at school like "To kill two birds with one stone," Mom would lose her shit and say, "Don't blame nature for your lack of ability to achieve two things at the same time! Oh mon Dieu!" And then she'd offer her new, more peace-loving proverb, "Hatch two birds with one egg."

At the end of the day, my mother's humor is what's allowed her to help hundreds of people in their recovery process—and hatch two birds with one egg!

Humor often springs from discomfort, fear, and self-doubt, and yet it is capable of healing discomfort, fear, and self-doubt. Use it.

DON'T BLAME THE LETTUCE

The quote at the beginning of this chapter, "When you plant lettuce, if it does not grow well, you don't blame the lettuce," comes from Thich Nhat Hanh's book *Peace Is Every Step*, and he continues by saying: "You look for reasons it is not doing well . . . Yet if we have problems with our friends or family, we blame the other person. But if we know how to take care of them, they will grow well, like the lettuce."

How many times (a day) do we blame the lettuce? A colleague, a friend, a spouse, the guy on line in front of us at a coffeehouse whose half-caf upside-down caramel drizzle latte took seven minutes to prepare and made us late and grumpy?

But the truth is that blaming has literally no positive or productive outcomes, whereas understanding and connecting bring us opportunities to learn and grow. So, instead of blaming your teammate for tanking his part of the presentation, try asking what he's got on his plate in order to understand why he wasn't better prepared. Instead of blaming your best friend for forgetting your birthday, try asking her if there's a reason she's been so distracted. Instead of walking through your life and office blaming everyone and everything when you fall short of excelling (You suck, stapler, it's all your fault we didn't get the account!), try asking yourself this: Do I want to cultivate more connections, understanding, and growth—or a rotten head of lettuce? Go to the source, find out what's going on, and let understanding set you free.

LET UNDERSTANDING SET YOU FREE.

BECOME THE RUBBER

When we are the object of blame, it's hard to maintain a spirit of imagination and creativity. And when people are literally calling us out, getting up in our face, and telling us that we really effed up on x, y, and z . . . it's kinda hard not to take it personally. But just as you have the choice to blame others for your problems or not, you also have the choice of whether to let blame stay stuck in your craw, or give yourself the Heimlich maneuver to dislodge it. It helps to remember that the reason why people look so upset, utterly terrified, and sometimes even red in the face when they are blaming you unfairly is because deep down they know they are really mad at themselves for effing up on x, y, and z and they don't yet have the courage to 'fess up, so they gotta aim the blame at you instead. We all blame and receive blame, so instead of internalizing the blame or taking it personally and letting it obstruct your creative process let it bounce off you. If you attended sixth grade, then you know exactly what to do! Adopt the mindset of a cheeky twelve-year-old and become the rubber. Repeat after me: *I'm rubber, you're glue. Whatever you say bounces off me and sticks to you!* After all, work can be sooooo sixth grade sometimes.

CHAPTER 18

TURN YOUR
VOCATION INTO A VACATION

> The real voyage of discovery consists not in
> seeing new sights, but in looking with new
> eyes.
>
> —MARCEL PROUST, *Author*

THE FIRST QUESTION customs agents ask you when you're traveling to or arriving from another country is: *Traveling for business or pleasure?* They don't ask you if you have heavy artillery in your carry-on, whether you plan on selling, buying, or eating drugs during your stay, or if you're part of a human trafficking ring. No, the most pressing question they have is whether you are traveling for business or pleasure.

A long time ago, I learned not to be honest when responding to this question. My answer always used to cause a kerfuffle. "Yes," I would say, to which the open-mouthed agent would respond, "Well, which one?" I would happily proclaim, "Both!" at which point I would be whisked away for further interrogation. Several missed flights and a handful of awkward strip searches later it finally sunk in: The idea that one might consider their *vocation* indistinguishable from a *vacation* makes authority figures profoundly uncomfortable.

Why do they even ask this question? Well, the guy on the

other end of the airline's customer service line might tell you that it's to gather "marketing insights" about how/why/where we travel, but I have another theory. They know that once more people start merging their vocation with their vacation, there is gonna be a serious work culture revolution and there are not enough TSA agents to stop it! Well, organizations, you better secure your borders, cuz us Creative Trespassers are coming to work and bringing all the curiosity, thirst for adventure, good humor, and focused serenity of a vacationer with us. The jig's up, customs!

You know how it is when you're on vacation and it's so easy to let go of all the bullshit you left on your desk, and it's like you're in a new mode—let's call it discovery mode—where you approach even the smallest things with a sense of wonder and joy? *I wonder why this drink has a green umbrella and my last one had a blue one? Ah, the pleasures of life!* And you know how, because you were able to let go of all the bullshit, you made room for all the cool shit, all the magic? Everyone you meet is friendly and interesting (and somehow knows someone from your hometown), the ice cream you eat is the best you've ever tasted, and when you show up at a charming restaurant you just kinda stumbled upon the hostess says, "You look so relaxed! Are you on vacation?" And you smile wide and say, "Yeah!" and she replies, "I've got a table just for you." And that table turns out to be the ONLY table with a window that looks out onto the clear blue ocean, and when the waiter comes to take your order he says, "You look so at peace. Are you on vacation?" and you proudly say, "Yes!" and he says, "Let me buy your next drink."

When you're on a vacation, life just shines a little brighter; even *you* shine a little brighter. Doors seem to open effortlessly, magic happens, and new experiences abound. Your body is relaxed, your senses are engaged, you're able to stop your mind from racing and be truly present in the moment. For many of us, vacations are the only times we get to truly reflect, learn, and explore.

In our work life, on the other hand, we rarely let go of the bullshit, rarely slow down so we can be present, rarely veer off the beaten path or allow our surroundings to surprise us anymore. But it doesn't have to be that way. You don't *have* to leave that sense of calm and focus at the all-inclusive resort. Vacation can be a mindset, one we can adopt when we get to the office every morning, only without the painful sunburn. This mindset can inspire us to continue to discover and explore and approach our work with new curiosity and wonder.

Once upon a time, I worked with a guy who wore grumpy pants from Monday through Thursday, but on Friday he came to work proudly donning one of his many Hawaiian shirts. Vibrant hibiscus flowers, palm trees and coconuts, surfboards and warm breezes; he had 'em all! For one glorious day each week, he was not a corporate drone, he was King Kamehameha, proud and confident, smiling at everyone, helpful but not intrusive. A born leader. However, this transformation was fleeting; as soon as the clock struck Monday, he was back to wearing his grumpy pants and a sour puss.

One of my favorite humans in the world, peace activist and Buddhist monk Thich Nhat Hanh, writes about achieving success in an illuminating way. In his book *The Art of Power* he says, "So the key to success is not the form of a monastic or layperson, of a police officer, a farmer, or doctor, but your capacity to cultivate happiness, understanding, and compassion."

It's never the job, the title, the uniform, or the outfit—no matter how colorful—that makes you successful, happy, or compassionate. There are as many unhappy CEOs as there are jovial cashiers, and there are as many pissed-off project managers as there are inspired marketing interns. It's not enough to wear a Hawaiian shirt on the outside if you're actually grumpy on the inside. The key is to wear your Hawaiian shirt on the inside, and not just on Friday. As Creative Trespassers, we know that we possess the power to make every day feel like a Friday; to merge our imagination with our vocation every day of the week.

When we learn how to approach our jobs with the sense of wonder, thirst for adventure, good humor, and focused serenity of a full-time vacationer, we can take those skills with us anywhere we go and anywhere we work.

There's a well-known study from Dr. Amy Wrzesniewski that shows how people who view their jobs as a vocation, rather than just some place they need to be to kill time until happy hour, are actually much happier and more fulfilled with the work they do. So, by viewing your vocation as a vacation too, you've got a shot at some next-level on-the-job fulfillment! It's time to get some V&V (vocation & vacation), because you deserve to be happier for way longer than an hour a day.

Perhaps you are reading this with a lil' bit of skepticism, wondering, "But what if my job sucks? What if I can barely manage to make it to lunchtime, let alone muster up enough gusto to sprint down the runway? What if the drudgery of answering phones, affixing parts, churning out content, serving other people and their priorities, feels more like indentured servitude than a vacation . . . then what, Katan?? HUH?"

The work that we're doing as Creative Trespassers isn't always easy; there aren't magic formulas for incorporating more joy into our work. Even wearing a Hawaiian shirt on the inside isn't a silver bullet. There will always be rude people, annoying inconveniences, and frustrating setbacks, just as there are on vacation. But you can choose whether to let them get you down or to turn those proverbial limes into margaritas.

When you're on vacation and it rains on the day you planned to go hiking, you don't get pissed off and curse out the hotel staff for ruining your day, do you? More likely you say, "Cool, I guess I'll go to a museum." And by turning a torrential downpour into a museum day, just like that, you've used a setback to enrich your creative life.

When you experience a shitstorm of setbacks or frustrations at work, you don't need to throw up your hands and accept them as your lot in life. Instead, you can choose to push up against them, harness them, and turn them into art. When we take this margarita mentality from our vacation back to work, even the most robust setbacks can fuel, rather than sap, our creativity.

Just take a page from a group of social entrepreneurs in Amsterdam who quite literally harnessed the storm clouds on the horizon to inspire an ingenious idea. Due to climate change, Amsterdam is receiving so much rain that certain parts of the city are at risk of flooding. So, these entrepreneurs came up with a creative solution: to collect the rainwater and turn it into beer.

USE SETBACKS AND FRUSTRATIONS TO FUEL YOUR AMAZING CREATIVE LIFE.

It's always going to rain. Instead of letting it ruin your vacation, why not use it to inspire your creative vocation?

CHOOSE THE JOURNEY, NOT THE JOB

Josh Greene couldn't make a living as a conceptual artist, so he followed in the footsteps of many a fine artist before him and took on two more jobs. One as a professor of art and one waiting tables at a fine-dining restaurant. Working in a restaurant was far from his dream job, but instead of complaining about how the work was so beneath him, or how much he hated having to walk around the dining room wielding a large wooden pepper mill and earnestly asking customers, "Would you like some pepper on your salad?" this quintessential Creative Trespasser found a way to bring more meaning to his less-than-creative service job by putting it in the service of the vocation he loved—art. That's when he came up with an art project called Service-Works. Basically, he gave away one night's tip money each month as a grant to fund other artists' projects. Because he worked in a super-high-end joint, those grants ranged anywhere from $100 to $450 a pop. That ain't chump change for an artist; in fact, that kind of money is significant enough to make the difference between an idea getting off the ground or not. And, in the super competitive (and often cold and institutionalized) world of applying for artist grants, the act of receiving one from a fellow artist, no matter the size, offers powerful encouragement and reassurance that one's ideas are worth investing in.

So now, when he offers customers cracked pepper and extra bread, Josh is also offering support to his fellow artists—while at the same time investing in his own art. He is, after all, a conceptual artist, which means the concept is, in fact, the artwork. And he's living proof that even our less-than-inspiring day jobs can inspire our amazing creative life.

BRING YOUR WEEKEND TO WORK

There are two questions I always ask clients upon meeting them for the first time: "What do you love doing?" and "When do you do it?" The first question yields the most amazing (and often unexpected) responses, especially from some seemingly buttoned-up peeps: I love playing guitar, cooking, reading poetry, writing screenplays, building furniture, making pottery, volunteering at animal shelters, restoring vintage cars, making homebrew, birdwatching . . . the list goes on. Then, without fail, everyone answers the second question with a resounding thud: On the weekends.

As Creative Trespassers, we don't need to relegate our creativity to the weekend. We can bring that part of ourselves into the workplace Monday through Friday.

I'm not suggesting you make hooch in the boardroom or keep a potter's wheel stashed in your cubicle. What I *am* suggesting is that playing the guitar, cooking up a storm, or restoring cars can inspire you to completely reimagine how you do your daily grunt work. Love weekend jam sessions with your friends? Why not bring a jam session of sorts to work? By that I mean, apply the same principles of rocking out to a team meeting, a common goal, or a brainstorming session. Just like when jamming with your friends, establish a vibe, a theme, and then riff! No set list, no right or wrong notes, just good ol' fashioned improvisation.

Whether you're answering phones and managing calendars, presenting ideas in front of colleagues or clients, or writing marketing copy, legal briefs, or code, finding the connection between the tasks you do at work and the creativity and passion you exert on the weekends will transform how you collaborate, solve problems, and make decisions. It will give you a fresh perspective on how to contribute with more imagination and gusto.

Bonus: You can also literally bring your weekend to work. Turn Hawaiian Shirt Fridays into Open Mic Mondays by hosting a lunchtime open mic where people can rock out, read poetry, share best beer-making practices, show photos of their refurbished car, or share inspiring stories from their volunteering work. Give each person a mic, five minutes, and an audience.

SCALE YOUR ENERGY

After I give a talk or lead a workshop, the number one thing people want to know is: *Where did you get all that energy?! How do I get some of that energy?* For years I've improvised weird answers on the spot: "From my mama!" or "I was just born this way!" Or "For breakfast I drink four cappuccinos and snort forty-four Pixy Stix." And then, of course, when I talk to tech start-up audiences, they don't just want to know how to get some more energy, they want to know how to "scale" that energy too. And I just want to scream, *I don't have a cloud-based solution for scaling human energy . . . I am a human being!*

The truth, though, has always been that I don't know where I get my energy, or why some people seem to just naturally have more energy than others. It always seemed like such an abstract concept to wrap my brain around. But as more and more people continued to genuinely want to know how to get more energy, I began to give it some serious thought.

Then it hit me: For years I've been de-siloing my life; fusing purpose with paycheck, creativity with productivity, vocation with vacation. My surplus of energy comes from the fact that I no longer have to constantly shift gears between creativity and drudgery, imagination and occupation, work and life.

Picture driving a stick shift with transmission problems, spitting and lurching into first, stalling in second, and having to ask your passenger to get out of the car and push so you can pop it into third. Now picture driving a brand-new electric car, where all you have to do is step ever so lightly on the gas pedal and you're moving forward, all the parts working in unison, no shifting gears, no weird sounds emanating from the motor or weird smells coming out of the muffler . . . That's what happens when there's no friction between what we do and who we are. That's the beauty of being a Creative Trespasser: We just put the pedal to the metal and watch our careers take off at full throttle!

So, if you want to scale your energy, stop compartmentalizing what you do, who you are, and what you're passionate about— and start finding qualities they have in common. Nothing, including YOU, works in a silo.

GO ON VACATION ALREADY!

A friend was once telling me that one of the benefits at his company is unlimited vacation. I said, "Hells to the yeah!" He said, "Hells to the no . . . as in, nobody ever takes a vacation."

WHAT?

That's like showing up for work and your boss left a slice of your very favorite cake on your desk with a napkin, fork, and sign that says "Eat up. You deserve it!" And yet you don't dare take a bite, for fear that people will find out that you're not just lazy but also gluttonous; that you don't work yourself to the bone, go days without sleep and sugary treats; that you don't *really* suffer.

To that I say: Don't be a martyr, that's so fourth century. Take your vacation already. I don't mean to sound like your mother, but do you know how many people around the globe don't get vacations? Are literally becoming ill because they are overworked and underpaid? If you have the luxury of taking a vacation, do it.

But that's not the only reason to take a vacation. If you don't do it for the sake of those who don't have that privilege, do it because no matter how much you might love your job, everyone needs to take a break every once in a while to refuel, relax, and reconnect with their vocation. Do it for the chance to bring back a gift to your colleagues that's even better than chocolate-covered macadamia nuts (although those are really good): the gift of a new perspective, fresh ideas, and a renewed spark.

And if you don't love your job, well, that's all the more reason to take a break. As my friend Melissa Lamson, global leadership coach and regular contributor to *Inc.*, says, "The best way to get unstuck in corporate culture is to leave it. Get outside of what you would normally do, go on vacation, find out what you're passionate about."

Productive Disruption

1. Get out your calendar.
2. Pick a week and mark it "vacation."
3. Get out a map.
4. Select a location.
5. Find a flight.
6. Book it.

CHAPTER 19

IF ALL ELSE FAILS . . .
KEEP REHEARSING

> Ever tried. Ever failed. No matter. Try again.
> Fail again. Fail better.
>
> —SAMUEL BECKETT, *Author and Playwright*

IT'S OPENING NIGHT of my one-woman show, *Saving Tania's Privates* (yes, you read that right), at the famed Edinburgh Festival Fringe in Scotland. I'm backstage in a tiny bathroom/dressing room/hallway awaiting my cue and obsessively going over my lines. *Did you say, "Can't, sir?" OH, can-cer! I have cancer?* The show is about my experience being diagnosed with breast cancer twice before the age of thirty (hey, what can I say, I'm an overachiever), coming out as a lesbian, running topless 10Ks after two mastectomies, and other run-of-the-mill stuff. After months of writing, rewriting, second-guessing, and rehearsing with a small-but-mighty team comprised of a kick-ass director, producer, stage manager, and dramaturge, it is time for the show to go on.

The sounds of a muffled intercom announcing last-minute gate changes and the hurried footsteps of travelers running late fill the theater. A disembodied voice announces the next flight: That's my cue! I sprint onto the stage dragging an uncooperative rolling suitcase behind me, when all of sudden, I'm under a spotlight. The team of imaginary TSA guards has misread my gender and sent a man to pat me down. As I assume the patting-down position (arms extended, legs spread out, you know, the ushe), I utter my first line. "Sir, why are *you* patting *me* down?"

The scene concludes, and the harsh glare of the spotlight gives way to a warm wash of light filling the stage and spilling out into the audience. I look out into the house and meet the curious gazes of those who, for the next eighty minutes (no inter-mission), will go on this epic journey with me: through love, loss, breast cancer, and partial nudity. What the audience doesn't know yet is that in the final moment of the show, I'll be taking off my shirt, exposing two mastectomy scars, and extending my arms out to the sides as if I am a human airplane about to take flight. And . . . Scene! BLACKOUT. The end.

On this particular evening, however, that "audience" (and I use the term loosely) consists of three people. One guy is asleep, another is clearly drunk and well on his way to being asleep, and one, bless his heart, seems like he is fully conscious and genu-inely excited to see the show.

If only I was the main character of a Choose Your Own Ad-venture book, this would be that hair-raising moment when I would get three magical options for escaping the impending disaster of having to perform a one-woman play about boobies (well, kind of) for an audience of three men.

   a. *If you decide to break down and cry onstage, turn to page 23.*
   b. *If you decide not to perform the middle sixty minutes of the show so you can get the hell out of there as quickly as pos-sible, turn to page 54.*
   c. *If you decide to lose your shit onstage and instead of taking off your shirt take off everything and scream, "Wake up, you drunken fools!" turn to page 13.*

What did I choose? I chose the fourth option: give it my all. There was no other choice, really, because in theater we learn early on that it's our job to show up and put on the best damn show we got in us, whether there are three people in the audience or three thousand.

Sure, it's awesome to perform in front of a full house of eager theatergoers who are rooting for you from the start of the show, but the reality of putting on seven shows a week is that sometimes you're going to look out into that ocean of empty chairs (and a couple of napping drunks) and feel like a failure. You're going to want to throw up your hands, run away, and give up. But whether you are performing onstage at a theater festival, in a conference room in front of your team's newest clients, or even alone in your office, tirelessly working on a big project, failure is never the goal, trying is. It's all necessary practice—or what us drama club kids call "rehearsal."

Fear of failure is one of the biggest obstacles when it comes to embracing our creativity. But this fear comes from a manufactured mythology that suggests that most innovative ideas, groundbreaking inventions, and imaginative art happen on the first try. The reality is that instant success takes years of learning, practicing, rehearsing, rewriting, rebuilding, and so on. Artist Louise Bourgeois was making art for over forty years before she became an instant success. By the time the press proclaimed writer Sandra Cisneros an overnight literary star, she had been developing her writing voice for years and years. And our favorite badass, Jen Sincero, didn't become a number one *New York Times* bestselling author until three years after her third book hit the stands.

We've all heard the rallying cry of entrepreneurs, the mantra of start-ups, and, increasingly, well-established corporations that goes something like: FAIL! *Fail often. Fail fast. Fail faster.*

Fail better. Fail more. Turns out, the business world borrowed this mantra from theater, more specifically from the playwright Samuel Beckett, who wrote, "Ever tried. Ever failed. No matter. Try again. Fail again. Fail better."

That somber dude understood that failure is part of life. He wrote about characters who were profoundly stuck; stuck up to their necks in a pile of scorched earth, stuck waiting on a train platform for someone who never shows up, stuck in indeterminate space and time. Beckett knew that living in the world meant getting stuck, but he also believed that we should never stop trying. And failing. And trying some more. He knew that the true art is in the messy failures that come before the exquisite outcomes.

Whether we receive a standing ovation, forget our lines, are booed off the stage, or have a drunk person pass out on the lip of the stage during our performance (not that this happened to me; I'm just saying), the minute we take the risk to get up onstage . . . we already succeeded. Success is the act of trying in the face of failure.

Of course, this isn't just true for theater and other strictly "creative" fields. We all fear failure to some degree, no matter what it is we do for work. Sometimes your résumé will kick ass but you won't get an interview. Sometimes you'll pitch your heart out and won't get the account. Sometimes your super brilliant idea for a business will be too early or too late. But don't despair, anyone can adopt what I like to call theater thinking, which goes something like this: *If no one shows up to your show . . . it's a rehearsal!* In other words, treat each "failure" as an opportunity to learn and improve. Comedians call this rewriting. Athletes, lawyers, doctors, and artists call it practice. Software developers call it beta testing. It doesn't matter what you call it—as long as you show up and risk being creative at work in the face of obstacles, resistance, and rules, it's impossible to truly fail.

Is there a creative idea you've been wanting to try, either in your job or in your everyday life? Something bold? Something that may sound a little crazy? Something that scares you? Something that has the potential to change the game, if only you could take the leap and try it? If so, there's no time like the present! Here are some tips to get you started.

QUESTION REJECTION

Rejection's just another word for nothin' left to lose! As a playwright, I was trained extensively in the art of receiving rejection letters. *Dear Tania, we received over five hundred submissions and . . . Sorry to inform you, yours has not been selected . . . We hope you'll consider submitting next year.*

The many, many letters of this nature that I received over the years were good preparation for my entrance into the workforce, upon which I began receiving many letters that sounded eerily familiar: *Dear Tania . . . Thank you for your application for the position of . . . As you can imagine, we received a large number of applications . . . I regret to inform you that you have not been selected . . . We encourage you to look at future opportunities . . .*

At first, my fragile young ego saw letters like these as a gigantic door being slammed in my face; clearly these people didn't understand my brilliance! But eventually (thank the Lord) I leggo my ego and was able to see these letters through a different lens. I realized that a rejection can be a slammed door in your face—or it can be the start of a conversation. You get to decide. The typical response is to take a rejection at face value, lick your wounds, and move on, but I decided to take a different approach. For example, when I got a letter from a coordinator at SXSW (South by Southwest) Interactive informing me that they had rejected my late submission to participate as one of their speakers, instead of dropping the letter directly into the paper shredder, I used it as an opportunity to start a dialogue. *Who are THEY anyway?* I thought. They're just human beings like I am, looking for the right fit. So I emailed back asking if one of the programming supervisors would be interested in speaking with me.

Although I didn't get the speaking gig, this was absolutely a pro move. Here's why: They responded to my email, letting me know how I could improve my submission for next time (for starters, apply on time) and promising to keep an eye out for it. In the end, I learned how to hone my pitch, while also making a memorable impression that in the future would help me stand out from among the hundreds of other submissions.

So, next time you are rejected or passed over for a job, a project, a gig, or anything else, instead of burning your rejection letters in effigy, use them to start a conversation. Ask for feedback, offer supporting materials, do your homework, and let them know why you're an awesome fit.

One caveat: If the answer is still no, respect people's responses. Persistent is one thing, but pushy is entirely another. And be gracious in all your correspondence. When trying to get past gatekeepers, you'll catch more breaks with honey than you will with vinegar.

Even if we're totally rocking it in our career, we'll all be rejected from *something* at some point or another. In fact, if you never get rejected, you are probably playing it way too safe. Those Creative Trespassers who are brave enough to approach a rejection as a conversation rather than a slammed door will become the great artists, influencers, and entrepreneurs of tomorrow. After all, do you want your tombstone to read: *She never tried, she never failed, but no matter . . .*

Or do you want it to read: *She showed up, she started remarkable conversations, and she made her mark!*

BETA TEST YOUR LIFE

When I started working in the software industry, I learned about beta testing. Beta testing is part of the development process and an awesome way for developers to get feedback from the actual people who will use their product before they actually launch it! With the feedback, they are able to refine the software, making it even more user-friendly than before. That's when I realized that making software is a lot like life; it's about constantly trying, evaluating, listening, learning, and refining.

Instead of thinking about our wackiest and most outrageous ideas or our most freakout-inducing decisions as BIG, scary, binary propositions—*win or lose, applause or boos, fail or succeed*—we can look at them as a beta test, a trial. You aren't making a lifelong commitment. It doesn't have to be perfect. You're just putting yourself and your idea out there and seeing how people respond. Then you take that feedback and you use it to do things better next time.

PRACTICE ABSURDITY

Thinking creatively is a skill just like any other. Doing it well takes practice. So, any time you feel like you're getting rusty, try this playful exercise: Give yourself or your team ten minutes to come up with ideas for the most absurd apps (or some other type of product) you can imagine! Here are some apps I made up while doing this exercise with team members at various companies. Yes, they are wacky, and yes, I'm a little freaked out to show you how nutty my brain is, but that's the point. You've gotta get comfortable putting your weirdest, craziest ideas out there, even if you're convinced that they stink. Because who knows; with the benefit of an outside perspective, you might come to

206 CREATIVE **TRESPASSING**

see that the idea you thought was the suckiest is actually kind of great.

> **Airdnd** *(Airbnb meets Dungeons and Dragons): Book underworldly accommodations all over the globe*
> **Tagline:** *Live like a gargoyle*

> **About̶F̶aceBook:** *For people who want to leave Facebook but still need a place to complain, brag, or selectively remember friends' birthdays.*
> **Tagline:** *Disconnecting never felt so social!*

> **Instagramp:** *See photos and videos from your grandfather's electrifying life! Tube socks and Gold Bond<3! #39cent Coffee #TSAIKeepMyShoesOn! #IGetToGoToDayCareToo #TheyGotMyLicenseSoIDrinkEveryNight.*
> **Tagline:** *I can't hear you . . . Show me a photo!*

PUT IT TO THE TEST

When I met Michelle Player, director of software quality assurance for *National Geographic*, she appeared to be pretty serious, task-oriented, and professional on the outside. However, it turns out that on the inside, she's a legit Creative Trespasser who's come up with a brilliantly sneaky way to gather feedback from her colleagues and team. Long ago, she suspected that whenever she sent her team a long email, they weren't reading the whole thing. So, she started sneaking in a little quiz at the very bottom of the email, with questions pertaining to the content of the email and a few left-fielders to make 'em laugh: *What is the difference between quality assurance and quality control? What did you think about our new automation tools? What is the real name of the cantina where Obi-Wan and Luke meet Han and Chewie?*

If you're testing out a new process, idea, or solution and need feedback from your entire team, try putting a quiz to the test! It's a fun way to elicit unvarnished insights, as well as to encourage focus and follow-through.

LEAD THE CHARGE ON CHANGING YOUR MIND

Have you heard the terms "growth mindset" and "fixed mindset"? If so, hang tight. If not, meet one of the world's leading researchers in the field of motivation, Carol S. Dweck. Early in her career, Dweck was obsessed with finding out how people coped with failure, so she designed a study for little kids. She gave 'em puzzles to solve that were way beyond their ability, knowing, of course, that they would fail. And indeed they did, but it was their *reaction* to that failure that led Dweck to a startling discovery: Some of the children actually LOVED trying to solve the impossible puzzles. They loved the challenge, loved stretching their minds, loved searching for solutions they had never thought of before; in short, they loved learning. To these kids, an impossible task was actually an opportunity to learn. She came to call this way of thinking a growth mindset.

Then there were other children in the study who gave up quickly, and still others who didn't try at all. Why? Because they were sure they would fail and didn't want to look stupid or silly. This way of thinking came to be called a fixed mindset. Eventually, Dweck's research showed that children, adults, schoolteachers, leaders of major corporations, all of us, have the ability to cultivate a growth mindset. The choice is ours.

Creative Trespassers know that regardless of where we fall on the organizational chart it's better to have tried and failed than never to have tried at all. Remember the first rule of Creative Trespassing: *Champion calamities, flaws, and profoundly awkward moments, knowing that these are where the best art, ideas, innovations, and life live!* Only when we begin to see our flaws, our mistakes, and our failures as opportunities to learn do we begin to take bolder risks, attack tougher challenges, and inspire those around us to do the same.

Productive Disruption

1. Ask a difficult question that no one else is asking.
2. Take on a challenge that seems impossible.
3. Stretch yourself further than you think you are capable of.
4. Practice looking at setbacks as opportunities for growth.
5. Help instill this mindset in others.

CHAPTER 20

PAY ~~YOUR DUES~~
ATTENTION

"Do stuff. Be clenched, curious. Not waiting
for inspiration's shove or society's kiss on your
forehead. Pay attention. It's all about paying
attention. Attention is vitality. It connects you
with others. It makes you eager. Stay eager."

—SUSAN SONTAG

EXIT INTERVIEW

What types of articles were you asked to work on during
your internship here at the magazine?

*If by "what types of articles" you mean what kind
of coffee creamer I was asked to procure for the
legitimate magazine staff members: Half & Half.*

Briefly note new skills, techniques, and knowledge
gained in this position.

*Filing back issues of magazines (sometimes with eyes
closed). Picking up cups and napkins for events. Filling
the coffee maker with water. Opening and sealing
mail with and without a letter opener.*

Were you encouraged to develop and pitch ideas for magazine articles?

Depends on how you'd define "encouraged." During one pitch meeting, I did offer an idea, which I thought was pretty good and then the second I said it, a staff member said, "Interns don't pitch," to which I responded, "Well, I just did!"

Would you recommend this internship to other aspiring writers?

See above.

THIS LITTLE GEM is an actual exit interview from my first (and last) internship. There I was, a bright-eyed and bushy-tailed twenty-something, working at a cool lifestyle magazine in San Francisco: a huge opportunity for an aspiring writer like me. And yet, instead of absorbing all the information I could about how to pitch an article, the basics of web design, or how to run an Internet-era media business, I was too busy complaining that my creativity was being squandered on what was, in my view, pointless grunt work that could just as easily have been performed by your average reasonably intelligent sloth.

Instead of using the opportunity to hone my journalistic voice (I was, after all, a writing intern), I was more concerned with using my voice to make sarcastic jabs at pitch meetings, to mock responsibilities that I deemed beneath me, and to tell anyone who would listen how the magazine could really benefit from my writing talents—not just my filing acumen. In other words, I was acting like a total jerk. But while you wouldn't know

it given my smart-alecky comments and borderline insubordi-
nate behavior, I was actually really excited to be interning at a
magazine that I loved and was eager to contribute creative ideas.

In hindsight, I was acting out because I had assumed that
interning at a creative company would guarantee that I would be
doing, you know, creative stuff. I expected that, even as a lowly
intern, I would be encouraged to speak up and share ideas, right
from Day One.

The insight that I lacked at the time was that those less-than-
thrilling tasks—like filing, archiving, and opening mail—are actually just as critical to the creative process as writing an article.
I now know that in order to produce a creative work, you have to
start out by doing the stuff that might seem less creative. Because
once you start to understand how every task—however mundane
it might seem—fits into the bigger picture, suddenly you stop
seeing those tasks, as stupid busy-work and start seeing them as
golden opportunities to learn.

There's a creative trespasser I know who works as an assistant
in a "creative" field; one she is passionate about and one in which
she could see herself someday forging a fulfilling career. And
yet, when I asked her to describe the vibe of her job, she let out a
deep, dramatic sigh and said, "I'm just serving my time." Whoa!
Nothing like an allusion to prison to get you good and disillusioned about your work. The problem, she told me, isn't so much
the scheduling and the photocopying and the coffee fetching
that her newly minted liberal arts degree totally overqualifies her
for. It's more that her head is bursting with creative ideas she is
dying to share, but as a member of the bottom of the food chain,
she is afraid to speak up, step out of bounds, or step on any toes.

Unfortunately, many office cultures—even very creative
ones—have an attitude of "interns and assistants should be seen
but not heard." There's a sense, when starting out in the working

world, that first we must "pay our dues" if we want to ever ascend to a position in which we can actually flex our creative muscles. After all, no matter what field or industry we choose to work in, we all have to start somewhere, and that somewhere is almost inevitably as an intern or assistant.

So, what do you do when your head is bursting with great ideas, and yet the office norms strongly suggest you keep your pie hole shut? You find the middle ground between honoring your role and using your voice—while cleverly sneaking in some creative ideas at the same time. Here are some strategies to try.

Productive Disruption

1. Pitch your supervisor on the idea of having one pitch meeting per year (or quarter) that is open for interns and assistants to pitch their ideas.

2. Let your creativity run wild . . . in your journal. Sometimes we can't share our ideas aloud, but we can certainly write them down. Get a journal or notebook. Keep it on your desk (or in a drawer), and when you can't contain your awesome ideas (and it isn't the time or place to share them), write them down, flesh them out, and have them ready for when it's your turn to shine.

3. Promise never to forget what it's like to be an assistant or intern, so that once you move up the ladder and begin managing assistants and interns you'll understand the balance that is needed to nurture the next gen of creative trespassers!

WRITE IT ON SPEC

It is common practice for aspiring screenwriters to write an entire episode of a television show or an entire screenplay for no money, with no one actually waiting to read it and a low probability that anyone ever will. The writer is investing their time, energy, and best jokes in a script that might never even make it onto a producer's desk; why?

Because instead of hanging out in L.A. coffeehouses chatting up producers in hopes of getting the elusive "big break" or sweating it out in the mailroom waiting to be "discovered," writing a spec script is active, not passive. It allows you to demonstrate that you have good ideas and the fortitude to develop and finish them. And, who knows, maybe your script does someday make it into the right hands, and those hands offer you a job writing on a show or buy the script outright. Or maybe not. Either way, it's a chance to take matters into your own hands rather than waiting around for an invitation to share your voice.

You can apply this idea in just about any type of job or field. When I've interviewed prospective interns and new employees for positions in marketing, graphic design, and even software development, I've given them a creative assignment on spec. They will not get paid for finishing this assignment—they might not even get the job—but it gives me a chance to see what's important to them, how they generate ideas, and whether they are motivated to finish a project even when they aren't technically getting compensated for it. In the end, even if the person isn't the right fit, they get to keep the rights to their work (as well as the work itself), add it to their portfolio, and use it for another opportunity. They also get a chance to challenge themselves, showcase their skills, and experience the actual turnaround time that would be expected of them in that job.

Tons of creative industries make spec work part of the hiring process. If you're a designer, you might find yourself rushing home after an interview to design a brochure, logo, or poster on spec. If you're trying to get into an editorial department at a publishing company, they might ask you to write a Reader's Report on spec as part of your interview process. Basically, you'll have twenty-four hours to read a book proposal or manuscript the publishing company is considering, and write the best book report your inner fifth grader can muster up. This gives them a window into how you write, how you think, and how you evaluate projects—and it gives you a chance to show off your mad skillz.

Once, I was a finalist for a senior director position at an innovation lab. You'd think that, at that level, I had already proven myself. Alas, I was given an assignment on spec to outline an action plan for my first six months on the job. It was due the following week. So, in addition to, you know, working at my current place of employment, I stole time on lunch breaks, mornings, and even on airplanes to brainstorm ideas, initiatives, and actions I could bring to the position over a six-month period. Before I turned in my assignment, I looked at it and thought, "This is awesome! They would be lucky to have me!" In the end, they disagreed. I didn't get the job but I did get to keep my action plan and use it as a kind of a map that ultimately led me to my next awesome position.

You don't need to wait until you're up for a new job or promotion to take your creativity out for a test drive. Remember, this is about being proactive. And even if you don't get to pitch your script, your proposal, your business plan, your article, (or anything else), nobody's stopping you from writing it, designing it, or developing it. And it's a good way to get your creative mojo flowing, regardless of what ultimately happens.

FIND THE JOY IN THE JOURNEY

While emceeing an event, I once had the privilege of meeting—and introducing—a real-life rocket scientist, Amber Gell. At the time, Gell was working with NASA—no joke—on designing and building the Orion spacecraft. So, we're hanging out backstage, shooting the shit, and she's telling me how it's been her dream since she was a little girl to be launched into space, and how she trains every single day in order to be ready for space travel. So, I'm like, "Cool! When are you going?" And she's like, "Oh, I may never go." And that's when the needle on my mental record screeched to a stop and I'm pretty sure I screamed, "WHAT?!"

Amber smiled as if she's heard that reaction before, and explained how there are so many factors that go into being chosen for a space mission that, no matter how much she trains and prepares, it's very possible she may never get the call. And just as I'm wondering how it would feel to devote your entire life to something that you might not ever get to do, she reads my mind and says, "I get to do what I love every single day. If I get the call, great; if not, I'm just getting better and better at what I love doing."

That's when it clicked for me. It's like painting or writing or singing; we may never get the call from the gallery or the publishing house or the record producer, but still we continue to create and get better at what we love doing.

In today's outcome-obsessed culture, where checklists, life hacks, and the never-ending quest for "inbox zero" seem to rule, there's something pretty magical about getting to do something you love, every day, with no particular goal or objective other than to experience the joy it brings you.

BECOME A MASTER APPRENTICE

Back in the day, mid-1400s to be exact, there was a master painter named Domenico Ghirlandaio known for painting detailed frescoes in churches and chapels all over Italy. Like a lot of other master artists and craftspeople of that time, Domenico enlisted the help of apprentices, young people who aspired to someday paint in churches and chapels too.

Sure, he asked the apprentices to do less creative stuff, like mix egg yolks and colored pigment to make tempera, or find a pig and then pull out a chunk of its hair to make a paint brush, but at the same time they were learning the skills necessary to paint a masterpiece, and getting the experience necessary to be—someday, at least—a master painter.

When you think about it, most entry-level jobs or internships (and even higher-level jobs, for that matter) can be treated like an apprenticeship. Next time you're feeling frustrated by all the noncreative tasks you need to get done at your job, focus on paying close attention to the "masters" around you, and try to soak up all the learning you can about your field and the skills needed to advance in it. That was the strategy one of Ghirlandaio's apprentices used, and, well, let's just say that Michelangelo ended up doing pretty well for himself.

TURN DRUDGERY INTO INSPIRATION

When I was younger, I spent years selling crap, bagging stuff, serving junk, slinging things, and filing files—all to pay the bills and leave me enough time to write and be creative. Every morning I'd wake up at 5:00 a.m. and work on my plays, stories, and performances up until I had to be out the door and head into work. It was exhausting. So, I saved my pennies until I had enough to live on for four glorious months, and I kicked my day job(s) to the curb. Oh, the freedom, the lack of constraints, the absence of tension and conflict. It was . . . the worst! I'd complained about my day jobs being uninspiring, and now I was less inspired than ever.

For all of those years, I thought my day job was disconnected from my "real" creative work, but it turned out that I'd been absolutely wrong. All of the tension, unusual characters, hard or awkward conversations, epiphanies, emotional growth, celebrations, and unexpected obstacles I had experienced at regular ol' work provided the color and texture that made my plays, stories, and performances come to life! Without even realizing it, I had been using my day job as source material for my entire creative life.

Artists—from stand-up comedians to composers to poets to painters—are constantly looking out for those everyday events, conversations, and moments that could end up being the linchpin of their next great work. At the height of her career, instrumentalist, electronics whiz, and performance artist Laurie Anderson, for example, decided to get a job at McDonald's. If you've ever seen or heard one of Laurie's performances, you know that it's her ability to observe—and translate—the human condition that makes her work so intimate, unnerving, funny, and human. Being able to hide behind a counter, and in a uniform, gave her the perfect vantage point from which to freely observe.

The point is, we can all turn the everyday characters, conflicts, conversations, and observations we pick up at work into source material for our creative outside-of-work pursuits. So, when the drudgery of your day job appears to be robbing you of your imagination, don't just grit your teeth and bear it. Turn it into inspiration instead.

CHAPTER 21

SHOW
UP

Wanna fly, you got to give up the shit that
weighs you down.
—TONI MORRISON, *Pulitzer Prize–Winning Author*

AFTER YEARS OF bouncing around from job to job to unem-
ployment to the racetracks, my father finally landed a stable gig
as the director of transportation operations at the Long Beach
Airport. What this means is that when you got off the airplane
and needed a cab, my dad, a leathery guy with a good smile and
a no-nonsense attitude, would grab your bag, tell you to follow
him, and lead you to the first car available in the line of cabs.

For years I was embarrassed by my dad's occupation. When
friends asked me what my father did for a living, I would casually say, "He works at the airport," hoping they would drop the
subject, but inevitably, their eyes would light up as they would
inquire, "Oh, is he a pilot?" And I would say, "Not exactly," my
tone suggesting that I didn't want to chat about my father's professional life, which I didn't, seeing as I didn't think of it as much
of a profession or a life.

That is, until the time I flew into Long Beach and got to see
him in action. As soon as I got off the plane, I spotted my dad
walking around that tiny airport like he owned the joint. He took

me around to meet his coworkers, proudly introducing me to all the cabbies, who patted him jovially on the back as we walked past. Then it was off to meet the older ladies who volunteered at the information booth and who, as soon as my dad said, "Hey, this is my daughter," giggled and blushed in his direction. Then to the car rental representatives, who brought my dad snacks and showed him photos of their new grandchildren. As I waited for my father to get off his shift, I watched him cracking jokes with everyone at the airport, making people laugh, and happily ushering tired travelers toward yellow cabs. And each time the cab door closed, my dad would whack the hood, sending them ceremoniously on their way, as if to say "Have a great trip" in Cab-ese.

That's when I realized that my father had a profession after all. His profession is safely transporting weary passengers from one location to another. It's making them smile at the end of a long journey. It's helping them get to their destination in a strange city or back home to their family. In other words, he's just like a pilot. Only on the ground.

My dad never tried to hide what he did for a living, never acted ashamed or embarrassed or pretended to be anything other than what he was. He may not have gotten to wear the fancy blazer with the epaulets on the sleeves and the pin in the lapel, but he took just as much pride in his work as any pilot. And he taught me that as long as you bring your whole self to work every day, you've got a profession and a life to be extraordinarily proud of.

BRING YOUR MAGIC WITH YOU EVERYWHERE

Growing up, I thought I'd end up working on *Saturday Night Live*. From the time I turned sixteen years old, I'd lie about my age to sneak into comedy clubs and perform on open mic night. For me, comedy was serious business. I'd spend every spare moment I had studying how to write and perform by watching *SNL*, *The Young Ones*, *Monty Python*, *Kids in the Hall*, *In Living Color*, and *The Tracey Ullman Show*. And when I wasn't watching the greats—and taking copious notes—I was writing my own sketches and stand-up comedy routines. Humor became a powerful tool for me to confront and reframe my sometimes crappy childhood.

When daydreaming about my future profession, I'd always envisioned myself writing and performing on a sketch comedy show. That made sense because it perfectly matched the identity I was developing: writer, performer, outsider, dreamer. Someone who used creativity and humor to push audiences outside their comfort zones, engage in difficult conversations, and see the absurd in the familiar.

Eventually I realized that being a comedian was far from the only viable career option for someone like me; that humor was magic I could bring with me everywhere. Having a sense of humor was often the reason why I was hired by companies, because they saw how humor has the power to open doors and minds, help people arrive at new meanings, and lift everyone up.

And once I let go of preconceived notions of what my career "should" look like, that's when I found myself doing exactly what I had imagined: writing, performing, dreaming, and using humor and creativity to push people out of their comfort zones and see the absurd—and the beauty—in the familiar. This is exactly what I'm doing now.

So the stage isn't at 30 Rockefeller; it's speaking at tech companies, corporations, arts and culture centers, and conferences of all stripes. And the audience isn't people at home in front of their televisions; it's twelve-year-old girls yearning to become future tech leaders, and it's today's tech leaders wanting to disrupt the future. It's marketing professionals striving to find more creative expression for their ideas, brands trying to tell more authentic stories to their customers, Creative Trespassers from around the globe choosing to put the spark and the joy back into their nine-to-five. Humor, writing, performing, and dreaming are at the core of all of my work, and it is no less important or urgent or inspiring than being on *Saturday Night Live*.

HUMOR IS MAGIC
YOU CAN
BRING WITH YOU
EVERYWHERE.
USE IT.

When you let go of the belief that there is only one thing you can do or be, only one form your creativity can take, only one perfect fit for your skill set, you will see the expanse of opportunities all around you. The landscape is always changing, and as long as you dare to leap and trust yourself, you will always land on your feet. Every day brings with it new opportunities to practice leaping into the unknown.

Every time you choose to leap, I want you to know that you are not alone. One of the coolest things about being a Creative Trespasser is that the minute you let people sneak a peek at your inner rebel, or the moment you let your imagination leak out, that's when you find out that you're surrounded by Creative Trespassers who have been hiding in plain sight.

Your mission, should you choose to accept it, is to make every day Bring Yourself to Work Day. And by that I mean your whole self, warts and all. If you're not yet ready to show up for you, please consider showing up for us: your colleagues, your family, your communities. Because we need your courage, creativity, and relentless curiosity to show us how to be more courageous, creative, and curious too. We need you to show up with all your flaws, fears, dreams, doubts, and ideas. We need the skills you have and the ones you desire to develop. We need you to find and use your unique voice in the service of innovating, of questioning, and of elevating fellow human beings. We need you to take bold risks with the knowledge that the opposite of success isn't failure, but apathy. And that failure is a necessary condition for growth. And if you're trying, well, then you're never truly failing because you're in a constant state of learning, growing, and rehearsing. We need you to bring your magic and good humor with you everywhere you go, not just to work, but beyond. YOU are needed in your work, in your life, and in all the spaces in between.

EVERY DAY BRINGS WITH IT NEW OPPORTUNITIES TO PRACTICE LEAPING INTO THE UNKNOWN.

As it turns out, there was true wisdom in my parents' odd logic—the logic that helped me embrace my inner outsider and forge a unique path toward a totally kick-ass life: *Use your creativity, value imagination, question authority, gamble, and, above all, don't be ordinary.* Think of this logic as my parents' gift to you. Take it, use it, share it. Make it your own.

THE OPPOSITE OF SUCCESS ISN'T FAILURE, BUT APATHY.

Productive Disruption

1. Put down the book.
2. Trust in the unknown.
3. Take a small-to-large leap of faith every day.

Recommended Resources to Ignite Your Creative Spark

SYLLABUS: NOTES FROM AN ACCIDENTAL PROFESSOR
By Lynda Barry

When the unconventional and genre-defying cartoonist Lynda Barry was offered a conventional job as a college professor and asked to come up with her own course and syllabus, she had no idea what the hell to do. The rules and conventions of academia just didn't seem to compute. So, she decided to create a syllabus in the form of an active comic strip. This book is like an explosion of her most creative questions, exercises, drawings, experiments, and tips designed to help us wake up our unconscious and kick-start our creativity. It's like a map that leads to the heart of imagination itself. It's AWESOME.

PRACTICE: DOCUMENTS OF CONTEMPORARY ART
Edited by Marcus Boon and Gabriel Levine

Okay, so I swear I don't have stock in Whitechapel Gallery or MIT Press, but holy guacamole, they sure do produce some of the best books about contemporary artists and art movements. In this great collection you'll find the work of some of the most trespassery artists out there, ones who have turned their very existence into a creative practice that turns everyday spaces into transmogrifying opportunities. You'll meet artists like Tehching Hsieh, Linda M. Montano, Pauline Oliveros, and Adrian Piper, and learn about how some of the most powerful pieces of art are community-based conversations. When you're ready for your mind to be blown open, this is your jam . . . we're talking dynamite for the soul! And if you get the chance to see these artists' work in real life, do it.

WHEN THINGS FALL APART: HEART ADVICE FOR DIFFICULT TIMES
By Pema Chödrön

When stuff at work, in our lives, or even in the world seems to be falling apart, Chödrön, like your cool aunt, gives it to you straight: Instead of running away from anxiety, fear, and discomfort, she shows you the transformative nature of turning into painful situations. If you're going through tough times and want to embrace the groundlessness of being alive . . . pick this sucker up.

MINDSET: THE NEW PSYCHOLOGY OF SUCCESS
By Carol Dweck

As I've said before, if you want to engage in Creative Trespassing, you have to get on board with the mindset that any pursuit can be a creative one. And in order to do that, you have to be expansive in your thinking, learning, and actions. That's where Dweck's concept of "growth mindset" comes in. Dweck's insights and research into how we can see "failure" as an opportunity to learn and grow inspire us to lead our lives (and our teams and companies) with more empathy, creativity, and love.

THE FLUXUS PERFORMANCE WORKBOOK
Edited by Ken Friedman, Owen Smith, and Lauren Sawchyn

This baby is chock-full of "scores" from tons of Fluxus artists. Download it and get ready to be inspired to conduct performances anywhere, anytime. It even has one of my favorite scores from Ken Friedman:

CHEERS
Conduct a large crowd of people to the
house of a stranger. Knock on the door.
When someone opens the door, the crowd
applauds and cheers vigorously.
All depart silently.

WRITING DOWN THE BONES
By Natalie Goldberg

M'bible. It is absolutely no wonder why this gem has been in print and selling strong for over thirty years . . . it's AMAZING!! From the moment I picked it up as a nineteen-year-old, it's become part of my Inner Guidance System, showing me how to mine everyday life for the details and stories that abound. This book has helped me overcome doubts as a writer and human being, as well as show me how and why to take my creative life seriously and *unseriously* (i.e., with a sense of humor).

THE ART OF POWER
By Thich Nhat Hanh

I recommend this book to every corporate audience I find myself in front of. And, in fact, have given copies to many a colleague, boss, mentor, mentee, and friend. Hanh shows us that "success" and "power" aren't like possessions that we can buy or use to keep people down, but, in fact, are only attained through living in a state of joy, intention, compassion, and peace. Being present is a full-time job, and this book is the best officemate ever!

VISUAL INTELLIGENCE: SHARPEN YOUR PERCEPTION, CHANGE YOUR LIFE
By Amy Herman

Can you imagine using paintings, sculptures, and fine art photography to teach cops, CEOs, and FBI agents how to solve cold cases and difficult problems? That's exactly what Herman does for a living, and in her book she explains how visual art can help us see the things that most people miss, so that we can make new discoveries that might solve a case or a problem, and maybe even save a life. When I finished writing my book, I treated myself to reading this book and . . . holy collective consciousness, Batgirl! Herman confirmed what and how I've been thinking and doing in the world. Thank you, Amy.

THE ARTIST'S JOKE (WHITECHAPEL: DOCUMENTS OF CONTEMPORARY ART)
Edited by Jennifer Higgie

As a fan of humor and contemporary art, I really dig how there are many contemporary artists using humor as a powerful strategy to engage audiences with emotionally, politically, and philosophically charged issues. This book is about that: You'll learn more about Maurizio Cattelan (the escape artist) and others who have snuck humor into their art, including Jenny Holzer, Hannah Höch, Paul McCarthy, and more.

ORBITING THE GIANT HAIRBALL: A CORPORATE FOOL'S GUIDE TO SURVIVING WITH GRACE
By Gordon MacKenzie

Although it looks like a regular book on the outside, on the inside it's like a portal to an entire world of doodles, whimsical drawings, and real-life stories from Gordon's *three decades* working at the, ahem, "hallmark" of all corporate greeting card giants, and how he used extreme creativity to survive and thrive. When you need to be reminded that your creativity is critical to your success (and that of your company), pick up this book, flip open to any page, read, giggle, and repeat.

GRAPEFRUIT
By Yoko Ono

Yes, many of us know Yoko as the cool chick who got to go on tour with John Lennon; however, before John came on the scene, Yoko was already an artist of note who showcased her creativity as a pioneer of the Fluxus art movement. This book is full of her humorous, subversive, and poetic "scores," or instructions for finding art in our everyday lives.

THE GUTSY GIRL: ESCAPADES FOR YOUR LIFE OF EPIC ADVENTURE
By Caroline Paul

Okay, so this is a young adult book, but I say: Why do the kids get to have all the fun?! I love this book so freaking much because it's all about kicking fear to the curb and experiencing the unbridled exhilaration of living! Part fun illustrations showing how to do cool stuff (like how to turn milk cartons into a boat), part real-life stories of Paul's crazy adventures (sneaking onto and climbing the Golden Gate Bridge, in the middle of the night . . . ACTUAL TRESPASSING, FOR REAL), and part history lesson of lesser-known women adventurers, this book is ALL rope swinging, tree climbing, fear conquering! The perfect gift for yourself or the budding Creative Trespasser in your life.

ONE CONTINUOUS MISTAKE: FOUR NOBLE TRUTHS FOR WRITERS
By Gail Sher

What Creative Trespasser wouldn't love a book about the power of making beautiful mistakes? My copy of this book has traveled with me through time and space. It's a meditation on turning failures into successes just as much as it is a guide to practicing creativity through writing.

THE CREATIVE HABIT: LEARN IT AND USE IT FOR LIFE
By Twyla Tharp

I think it's safe to say that Twyla Tharp is a centuple threat: brilliant choreographer, award-winning dancer, creator of Broadway shows, and so many more creative accomplishments. If you want to have your socks blown off, you'll just have to go to her website and delight (www.twylatharp.org). Oh, and in her spare time . . . she wrote this book filled with all kinds of creative exercises to help readers make creativity a priority and a habit. After all, you don't become a triple (or centuple) threat without developing great habits.

Acknowledgments

THANK YOU. You amazingly generous, eternally creative, and delightfully unruly human beings who have aided and abetted my creativity, and supported me in sneaking it into book form. I thank YOU:

To Julie Grau and Adam Stern, Elizabeth Cutler and the entire Cutler family, Amy Silverman, Stacy Brunelle, Kristen Weber, Deborah Weir, Alison Wade, Julie Hampton, Ann and Tim Cothron, Chris Norwood, Rob Nicoletti, Eliza Woloson, Steven J. Tepper, Sherry Cameron, Dan Tyre, Aefa Mulholland, E.J. Bernacki, Bill King and Mary Lucking, and so many more. Thank you to the kindred spirits who contributed quotes, stories, insights, and shenanigans.

In addition to sharing initials, Talia Krohn and I share a sense of humor, a love of Salt-N-Pepa, and a desire to make the written word more inspiring at every turn. Talia has managed to turn the act of editing, something that could easily be rigid and lack imagination, into the most dynamic and joyful act of Creative Trespassing.

Speaking of joy . . . who wouldn't want to work with a sense of joy? And even better, an actual person named Joy?! To Joy Tutela, the agent who wooed me with Middle Eastern food and sealed the deal with deadlines, encouragement, and a wicked sense of humor—thank you.

Thank you to the entire Currency team! To Megan Perritt for putting the *public* back into publicity and helping to create events that are for and of the people, and to Ayelet Gruenspect for making marketing an opportunity to start a conversation.

To my dear friend Jen Sincero, thank you for cheering me on, paving the way, and always answering the question, *wassuuup*?!

To my wildly imaginative, super scrappy, and relentlessly supportive family, thank you for showing me how to champion the people, places, and ideas that are less recognized in our society so that I could take the road less traveled. That's made all the difference!

I know it's not traditional to thank forms, but these forms have invited creative sneakery to enter through the front door: Axosoft, SMoCA, Mod PHX, and The Coronado.

To the woman who inspires me to see the spaces in between and to live a life filled with curiosity, laughter, and art: Angela Ellsworth. To the man who keeps me down to earth by insisting I pick up his shit, Felix.

Thank YOU, Creative Trespassers, for taking imagination seriously and sneaking more of it into less overtly creative spaces and situations! I can't wait to see your productive disruptions!

Epigraph Sources

CHAPTER 2
The Creative Habit by Twyla Tharp (Simon & Schuster, 2003).

CHAPTER 4
Letters of Note: An Eclectic Collection of Correspondence Deserving of a Wider Audience compiled by Shaun Usher (Chronicle Books, 2014): "Do" by Sol Lewitt, to Eva Hesse, pg. 88.

CHAPTER 6
What's the Story: Essays About Art, Theater, and Storytelling by Anne Bogart (Routledge, 2014).

CHAPTER 9
The Rebel: An Essay on Man in Revolt by Albert Camus (Alfred A. Knopf, 1961).

CHAPTER 10
No One Belongs Here More Than You by Miranda July (Scribner, 2007).

CHAPTER 11
The Language of the Night: Essays on Fantasy and Science Fiction by Ursula K. Le Guin (Putnam, 1979).

CHAPTER 12
When Things Fall Apart by Pema Chödrön (Shambhala, 2002).

CHAPTER 14

Walking Art Practice: Reflections on Socially Engaged Paths by Ernesto Pujol (Triarchy Press Ltd, 2018).

CHAPTER 16

Feminism Is for Everybody: Passionate Politics by bell hooks (Routledge, 2014).

CHAPTER 17

Peace Is Every Step: The Path of Mindfulness in Everyday Life by Thich Nhat Hanh (Bantam, 1991).

CHAPTER 18

In Search of Lost Time, Volume I: Swann's Way by Marcel Proust (Modern Library, 1992).

CHAPTER 19

Nohow On: Company, Ill Seen Ill Said, Worstward Ho: Three Novels by Samuel Beckett (Grove Press, 1995).

CHAPTER 20

Song of Solomon by Toni Morrison (Alfred A. Knopf, 1977).

Index